P. Cezanne

Ulrike Becks-Malorny

Paul Cézanne

1839–1906

Pioneer of Modernism

TASCHEN

Contents

From Banker to Painter

"Paul may have the genius of a great painter, but he will never possess the genius actually to become one. He despairs at even the smallest obstacle."

This harsh criticism by Paul Cézanne's friend of his youth, Émile Zola, remained true of him throughout his life and his career as an artist. Deep inside, he had a belief in his own genius and a determination to pursue his artistic goals, and this belief remained unshaken by frequent periods of self-doubt and despondency. Another of Cézanne's traits was his refusal to make any form of artistic compromise or concession to society, and this often made him appear a strange and eccentric figure.

Cézanne lived only for painting; it was his sole passion in life, and family ties and friendships took second place as far as the "hermit from Aix" was concerned. He saw his surroundings through the eyes of a painter, studying the effects of light and shadow on objects and exploring the relationships between forms and colours. And life was a constant, tormented struggle. Cézanne was a self-taught artist who was rarely satisfied with the results of his labours. Each new picture was a source not so much of pleasure as of pain at his own failure to realize his ideas, so that quite frequently he destroyed a canvas in disappointment and rage at his own inability.

This excitable and impetuous nature was apparent even in Cézanne's youth. He was the least confident and most easily roused of three friends who met at the Collège Bourbon, the long-established humanist college in Aix-en-Provence. The other two were Émile Zola, the future novelist, and Jean-Baptiste Baille, who later became an engineer.

The three young men, known at college as the "Inseparables," spent their free time making long excursions in the surrounding area, hunting and fishing and swimming in the river Arc. They held endless debates about art, read Homer and Virgil together, and shared their enthusiasm for the Romantic authors Victor Hugo and Alfred de Musset. They took particular pleasure in writing poetry. Cézanne was an excellent pupil, and was particularly interested in the Classical languages: he often wrote his verses in Latin. "My verse may be purer than yours," Zola admitted to his friend, "but yours

PAGE 6
Louis-Auguste Cézanne, the Artist's Father, Reading L'Evénement, 1866
Oil on canvas, 198.5 x 119.3 cm (78¼ x 47 in.)
Washington, D.C., National Gallery of Art, Collection of Mr. and Mrs. Paul Mellon

The portrait of Louis-Auguste Cézanne as an old, serious and dignified man reveals nothing of the artist's humiliating dependence on his father until the latter's death.

is certainly more poetical, more true; you write with the heart; I, with the mind." He acknowledged that Cézanne's poems were more serious, but Cézanne regarded them simply as an agreeable pastime: he had no intention of becoming a serious poet.

Nor did Cézanne show any particular love of painting during this period of his life: he won many prizes at school for above-average performance, but gained only one award for drawing, in the year when he studied at the École spéciale de Dessin in Aix.

The three friends' carefree time together came to an abrupt end in February 1858, when Zola left Aix and went to Paris. As a result of the separation, Cézanne and Zola exchanged frequent letters, swearing undying friendship and recalling the hours they had spent together. Zola greatly missed Cézanne and urged his friend to follow him to Paris and begin a career as a painter. Zola had a very clear idea of how Cézanne might live his daily life in Paris:

"From six to eleven in the morning you could do life painting in a studio school; then you could have your lunch, and from twelve to four in the afternoon you could copy a masterpiece which particularly appealed to you in the Louvre or the Luxembourg Museum. That would mean nine hours of work. I think that would be enough, and with such a programme you are bound to make progress."

Zola was very aware that his friend needed a precise timetable of this kind: he knew that Cézanne was indecisive, lacked confidence, and was unable to stand up to his powerful, authoritarian father. Louis-Auguste Cézanne had worked his way up from a modest position as a hat salesman and exporter to become a successful banker in Aix, and he believed that his son's career lay in banking. He was a pragmatic businessman, obsessed with money and quite unable to conceive that his son might ever want to become an artist.

So Cézanne complied with his father's wishes and, after his school-leaving examinations, signed up for a course in law at the University of Aix-en-Provence. His father wanted him to work in his bank after completing the course.

Cézanne spent two years reluctantly studying law, yet he devoted every minute of his spare time to drawing and writing poetry. In 1859 he began evening classes in life painting at the École spéciale de Dessin in Aix, where he met his former classmates from the Collège Bourbon: Achille Empéraire, Philippe Solari and Numa Coste. At the school, housed in the Musée Granet, Aix's Museum of Fine Art, he won a second prize in the figure study painting course.

Cézanne was increasingly neglecting his law studies and devoting himself to art, and was often to be seen copying paintings in the Musée Granet. But his father still refused to allow him to go to Paris. Meanwhile, in the capital, Zola was growing impatient: he knew how indecisive Cézanne was and accused him of not trying hard enough to get what he wanted.

"Is painting only a whim that took possession of you when you were bored one fine day? Is it only a pastime, a subject of conversation, a pretext

Eugène Delacroix
The Barque of Dante, 1822
Oil on canvas, 189 x 241 cm (74½ x 95 in.)
Paris, Musée du Louvre

"The Barque of Dante," after Delacroix,
1870–73
Oil on canvas, 25 x 33 cm (10 x 13 in.)
Private collection

Cézanne painted a total of six copies after works
by the Romantic artist he so greatly admired. It
was from Delacroix that he learned to use colour to express the inner relationships between
figures and objects.

for not working at law? If this is the case, then I understand your conduct;
you are right not to force the issue and make more trouble with your family.
But if painting is your vocation – and that is how I have always envisaged
it – if you feel capable of achieving something after having worked well at it,
then you are an enigma to me, a sphinx, someone indescribably impossible
and obscure… Shall I tell you something? But do not get angry: you lack
strength of character. You shy away from any form of effort, mental or
practical. Your paramount principle is to live and let live and to surrender
to the vagaries of time and chance… If I were in your position, I would
make a decision and stake your all, instead of continuing to drift back and
forth undecided between two such different places as the studio and the
courtroom. It pains me that you suffer from this uncertainty, and I believe
that would be another reason to give your all. Either one or the other –
either become a proper lawyer, or become a serious painter, but do not
become an undecided creature in a paint-spattered robe."

Life in the Cézanne household had become increasingly intolerable.
In 1859, the family had bought Jas de Bouffan, the decaying former summer
residence of the Governor of Provence. Paul became increasingly with-
drawn, and eventually his father relented and allowed his son to leave Aix.
Cézanne went to Paris in 1861, where Zola eagerly awaited him.

But his great hopes of Paris were not fulfilled. He made frequent visits
to the Louvre, where he copied works by Titian, Rubens and Michelangelo.
He met Zola and regularly drew in the Académie Suisse, a studio where
young art students could work from models for ten francs a month.
It was there that he met Camille Pissarro, who was nine years older than
himself and with whom he later painted from nature, as well as Armand
Guillaumin, Claude Monet and Auguste Renoir. He also met Achille
Empéraire, whom he knew from the Aix Drawing School.

PAGE 10
Spring, c. 1860
Oil on canvas, 315 x 98 cm (124 x 38½ in.)
Musée des Beaux-Arts de la Ville de Paris,
Petit Palais

Summer, c. 1860
Oil on canvas, 314 x 109.5 cm (123½ x 43 in.)
Musée des Beaux-Arts de la Ville de Paris,
Petit Palais

The first pictures to be painted were probably
the inner two, *Summer* and *Winter*, since the
artist would appear to be less at home with
the new technique of painting in these two
works. The motifs on the outer walls, *Spring*
and *Autumn*, are more skilfully painted.

Nonetheless Cézanne was not happy in Paris: he still felt an outsider, and before long he was planning to leave. "I am wasting my time in every respect," he complained to a friend in Aix. "Just don't go imagining that I shall become a Parisian…"

Zola was disappointed by Cézanne's lack of drive, and tried to inveigle his friend into staying by asking him to paint his portrait. Cézanne did so, but was so disappointed by the result that he destroyed it. In September 1861, after his application to join the École des Beaux-Arts had been rejected, he returned to Aix, deeply disappointed.

There he reluctantly returned to work in his father's bank, but he also set up his own studio in Jas de Bouffan. No sooner was he back at his desk than he was longing to return to Paris. In the bank's account book, he wrote: "The banker Cézanne does not see without fear / Behind his desk a painter appears." His father realized that Paul would never take over from him at the bank and allowed him to travel to Paris a second time, this time on condition that he study properly at the École des Beaux-Arts. He gave his son a monthly allowance of 125 francs to enable him to work without having to earn a living.

Back in Paris, Cézanne was again turned down by the École des Beaux-Arts on the grounds that his paintings were clumsy and unconventional, a long way from what was generally regarded as art. Cézanne did not take his application any further, for he had had enough of the École des Beaux-Arts, with its rigid hierarchies and hidebound attitudes. Instead, he continued his studies at the Académie Suisse, which he now regularly attended.

The École des Beaux-Arts was the real pillar of the French artistic establishment at this time. It was impossible to imagine a successful career as an artist without it, and particularly without its associated annual

Paul Alexis Reading to Zola, c. 1869/70
Oil on canvas, 52 x 56 cm (20½ x 22 in.)
Private collection

This painting, built up using effective light-dark
and red-green contrasts, shows Cézanne's friend
from his youth, Émile Zola, author of the novel
cycle *Les Rougon-Macquart*. The other figure is
Zola's secretary Paul Alexis, a journalist, writer
and friend of Cézanne from his time in Aix.

exhibition, the Salon. Its high priest was the Classicist Jean Auguste
Dominique Ingres (1780–1867), and his serried ranks of pupils obeyed his
dictum that line was more important than colour: the main aim was to base
work in paint on very detailed drawing and careful outlining. Paint itself
was used simply to provide colouration. The canvases were dominated
by historical and mythological scenes; using landscape as a subject for
paintings in its own right was totally out of the question.

In the second quarter of the century, Eugène Delacroix (1798–1863) led
a Romantic backlash against this dictatorship of the line. The Romantics
regarded colour as more important than drawing, and the artist's individual
sensitivities as more important than artistic convention. As a result, the
French art world split into two camps. The battle between Ingres and

***The Orgy, or the Banquet**, c.* 1867
Coloured chalk, pencil, watercolour and
gouache on cardboard, 32.4 x 23.1 cm
(12¾ x 9 in.)
Private collection

Cézanne repeatedly depicted the themes of
the war between the sexes and of seduction.
The grainy colour of this particular painting
is reminiscent of a Venetian mural.

PAGE 15
***The Orgy**,* 1864–68
Oil on canvas, 130 x 81 cm (51¼ x 32 in.)
Private collection

Delacroix, Classicism and Romanticism, line and colour was a major topic
of discussion and a popular subject for caricaturists.

Alongside these currents, with their largely aristocratic and upper
middle-class roots, a new movement grew up using raw, unadorned real life
as its subject matter. It was founded by Gustave Courbet (1819–1877), whose
adherents called themselves the "Realists"; their battlecry was: "Let us be
true, even if we are ugly!" Influenced by the industrial and political revolu-
tions of the day, the artists began using subjects from contemporary everyday life, and Courbet called on them to paint ordinary scenes and figures,
to "bring art into contact with the common people."

But the final break with historical painting was made by Édouard Manet
(1832–1883), whose painterly version of Realism, with its bright, clear-edged
colours, was admired by the open-air painters. Manet was interested not
in analytical observation but in reproducing his own subjective perceptions,
freeing the subject from any burden of symbolic content.

The conflict between these different currents was the subject of much
impassioned debate in cafés and studios. The artists of the Académie
Suisse strongly advocated Realism and discussed the paintings of Édouard
Manet, while, in the Academy's narrow-minded École des Beaux-Arts,
artists adhered firmly to the tenets of Ingres. The middle-class public still
preferred large-scale historical paintings, allegorical scenes and insipid
genre paintings.

The most important forum for artists was the annual Salon, which was
largely the arbiter of public tastes. The Academy's members followed strict
criteria in selecting the entries: there was no place for originality, innovation
or anything which differed from the Academy style. But it was every artist's
greatest desire to be in the Salon, as this was the only way of exhibiting work
in public, gaining a reputation and selling pictures.

When a particularly large number of works were turned down at the
1863 Salon, there were massive protests from artists, with the result that
Napoleon III allowed a parallel exhibition to be set up for works which had
been rejected. This "Salon des Refusés" was intended to give the public
a chance to form their own views about the works which had been turned
down by the Academy.

But people were not at all used to the idea of making up their own minds
about contemporary art, and the exhibition was ridiculed. The criticism
centred on Manet's *Le déjeuner sur l'herbe* (1863, ill. p. 24), which Napoleon
III described as "indecent." The strikingly relaxed display of female nudity
in Manet's painting, set in a realistic landscape rather than the intimate atmosphere of a boudoir, scandalized the middle-class public. So did the sim-
plified, rapid style of painting, with its renunciation of any form of illusion:
as Zola wrote, "One is not accustomed to seeing such simple and sincere
renditions of reality."

The *succès de scandale* of the "Salon des Refusés" drew young painters
closer together. The Café Guerbois in the Batignolles district became
a regular meeting-place for Manet and his circle, and Cézanne often went

Incident du 20 mars au Palais de l'Industrie ou un succès d'antichambre avant l'ouverture du Salon

This caricature shows Cézanne with the two paintings that were rejected by the 1870 Salon.

there. But he remained an outsider to this environment. With his strong Provençal accent, dishevelled clothing, rustic appearance and distrustful personality, he did not fit in to the Paris art world, and he was mocked as an eccentric.

Paul Cézanne never stayed in one place for very long. Even in Paris he frequently moved apartments and could rarely tolerate the hubbub of the city for more than six months at a time, retreating instead to the Provençal seclusion of Jas de Bouffan. Between 1863 and 1870 he regularly spent part of the year in Aix, where he painted numerous portraits of his uncle Dominique, who willingly sat as his model.

It was there, as well, that he painted his portrait of *Louis-Auguste Cézanne, the Artist's Father, Reading L'Événement* (ill. p. 6). He showed his father immersed in a liberal newspaper of the kind which he would not normally have dreamed of reading; Louis-Auguste normally read the republican paper, *Le Siècle*. In fact *L'Événement* was the publication in which Zola regularly wrote articles defending Manet and his circle of young artists as well as condemnations of the jury at the 1866 Salon. On the wall behind his father is a still life by Cézanne, looking like a normal part of the furnishings of the house. This severe portrait, painted with a palette knife, flies in the face of reality by depicting Louis-Auguste Cézanne as a benign patriarch. Could this be an embodiment of Cézanne's wish for a harmonious relationship with his father, a relationship respectful rather than patronizing?

A few years later, Cézanne painted the *Portrait of Achille Empéraire* (1867/68, ill. p. 17), his fellow-student at the Académie Suisse, whom he greatly respected. Empéraire lived in extreme poverty; a hunchbacked dwarf, he never achieved recognition during his lifetime. The portraits of his father and Empéraire, each sitting in the same chair, were painted only a few years apart. A comparison shows how much Cézanne's style had changed during this short period: the flowery seat cover in the portrait of his father is painted in an Impressionist, illusionist manner, but the decoration on Empéraire's chair is shown very precisely, almost schematically. The strong frontal approach, the evenly lit picture with very few areas of shadow and the bold use of colour give the subject a monumental dignity. The painting grants this humble artist the recognition which so obstinately eluded him during his lifetime.

Cézanne submitted this painting and a female nude, which has since been lost, to the 1870 Salon. As usual, he was rejected. An article on the Salon by a critic named Stock includes a caricature of Cézanne and the two rejected paintings (ill. p. 16). Cézanne is portrayed as an eccentric-looking figure with a walrus moustache, and his two paintings are distorted and grotesque. Cézanne defiantly defended himself:

"Yes, my dear Mr Stock, I paint how I see, how I feel – and I have very strong feelings – you also feel and see as I do, but you do not take risks… You paint Salon paintings… I take risks, Mr Stock, I take risks… I have the courage to stand by my opinions… and… he who laughs last, laughs longest."

Cézanne and the Impressionists

When the Franco-Prussian War broke out in the summer of 1870, Cézanne moved from Aix to the fishing village of L'Estaque, near Marseilles, thus avoiding being called up. For the past year, he had been living with a woman eleven years younger than himself, Hortense Fiquet, a bookbinder whom he had met as a model in Paris. But this relationship did not bring him the freedom from loneliness and sexual frustration which he sought. Cézanne was shy in the presence of women and had a panic-stricken fear of physical contact, which he admitted was rooted in a childhood trauma: when he was at school one day, he had been standing on a staircase when another child suddenly kicked him violently from behind. He also distrusted other people, and none of these traits changed as a result of living with Hortense.

Cézanne kept this relationship secret from his father for eight years, afraid that his monthly allowance might be cut off. It was not until 1886 that he set the seal on his relationship with Hortense by marrying her.

Hortense did not share Cézanne's passion for painting and literature, and she preferred the bright lights of Paris to the solitude of the Provençal countryside. But she seems to have possessed huge reserves of patience and posed for the artist in endless sittings. He painted over forty portraits of her, mostly showing her as a severe and reserved-looking woman with hard, angular features, such as *Madame Cézanne in a Red Armchair* (c. 1877, ill. p. 40) and *Madame Cézanne in Blue* (1888–90, ill. p. 53).

In L'Estaque, the war seemed far away, and Cézanne, who had never been interested in the machinations of politics, remained wholly oblivious to it. He ignored his call-up papers and concentrated entirely on painting. He later said to Ambroise Vollard: "During the war, I worked a great deal from nature in L'Estaque. Apart from that, I cannot tell you of a single unusual event that occurred in 1870/71. I divided my time between the countryside and the studio."

Cézanne became intoxicated with the rocky Mediterranean landscape, and painted for all he was worth. He worked outdoors and made great efforts to depict only what he saw with his own eyes. The fishing village

19

of L'Estaque, with its greyish-green, mirror-like bay, the rows of houses and steep streets, the rugged white limestone crags and emerald-green pines, provided him with plenty of new subjects for his paintings.

Cézanne showed no reaction to the proclamation of the Republic. A new town council was formed in Aix and made him a committee member of the drawing school and the museum, a post in which he could have exerted an influence on the museum's policy. Like his father, who was elected to the finance committee but never attended a council meeting, Cézanne showed no interest in the public affairs of his home town. He remained in the fishing village and devoted himself to painting its magnificent landscape. After the winter of 1870/71, which was unusually cold and snowy by Provençal standards, he painted *Snow Thaw in L'Estaque* (*c.* 1870, ill. p. 22).

This painting is still largely dominated by the sombre colours, stark contrasts and dramatic exuberance of Cézanne's early work, but the subject is no longer a work of the imagination: it is painted from life. The steep diagonals of the snow-covered slope and the roof of the house are real, as are the tops of the stone pines bent by the Mistral and the threatening sky. But this drama of nature in the raw also reflects the artist's inner turmoil. Cézanne's passionate temperament was still causing him problems, and his technique did not enable him to depict what he saw in nature with sufficient detachment and rigour, and at the same time allow his own perceptions to resonate in his work.

Cézanne spent part of the war in L'Estaque with Hortense and part of it in his parents' house in Aix without her. It was there, near Jas de Bouffan, that he painted a prosaic southern French landscape, *The Cutting* (*c.* 1870, ill. p. 21). The bright colours and simple, unsentimental motif already show the influence of the bright colours of the Impressionists, but his style of painting is completely different from theirs. Cézanne has used broad, decisive expanses of colour which give the landscape considerable strength and formal rigour. Objects retain their own materiality: sand, earth and rocks are not hinted at, but are presented to us as direct, banal, unadorned reality. The almost parallel arrangement of the individual planes leads the eye to the centre of the picture, where the railway cutting slices into the picture like a gaping wound.

Cézanne often voiced his attitude to the changes which technological progress had wrought in the landscape and in people. "The town of Aix has been ruined by the Chief Engineer of Roads. You will have to hurry if you want to see anything. Everything is disappearing," he remarked to his fellow-painter Émile Bernard. And he told the archaeologist Jules Borély: "Above all other things, I love the look of people who have grown old, but have not departed from their traditional ways in accepting the laws of the time. I hate the effects these laws are having."

In view of this assessment, the bald, emotionless painting of the railway cutting with its mountain, fields and hills can be seen as an invocation of the eternal and constant dominance of the powers of nature. These powers provided a counterpart to the changes wrought by time. This painting also marks the debut of Cézanne's much-loved mountain, Mont Sainte-Victoire, a massive, almost surreal prominence with its crystalline structure providing a symbol of timelessness and permanence.

After the war ended, Cézanne and Hortense returned to Paris, where their son Paul was born in January 1872. Cézanne was discontented and angry with himself and the world: he had a family to feed, and was more tied down than ever before. His friend Achille Empéraire asked to stay with him for a few months, but left Cézanne's apartment in the Rue Jussieu after only a short time:

"… it was unavoidable; otherwise I would not have escaped the fate of the others. I found him here, abandoned by everyone. He hasn't got a single intelligent or close friend any more. Zola, Solari and all the others are no longer spoken about. He is the strangest chap one can imagine…"

During this despondent period, Cézanne took up Camille Pissarro's invitation to visit him in Pontoise. There, in the Oise valley, where Charles François Daubigny had also settled, there were countless subjects for landscape painters. Cézanne was delighted at the invitation, since he still lacked the experience to develop the individual technique which he needed. This he hoped to learn from Pissarro.

The fact that the shy and sensitive Cézanne was able to put himself in someone else's hands probably reflected Pissarro's sympathetic and tolerant personality. He had a patient and unassuming nature which made him a born teacher. "Pissarro was like a father to me… almost like the good God,"

The Cutting, c. 1870
Oil on canvas, 80.4 x 129.4 cm (31¾ x 51 in.)
Munich, Neue Pinakothek

Cézanne painted this ordinary-looking landscape near Aix in the bright colours of the Impressionists, but without creating atmosphere by resolving the forms. This is the first of his paintings to feature the mountain he loved so much, Mont Sainte-Victoire.

Snow Thaw in L'Estaque, c. 1870
Oil on canvas, 73 x 92 cm (28¾ x 36¼ in.)
Zurich, Stiftung Sammlung E. G. Bührle

The expressive drama of this landscape is reminiscent of the highly emotional figure paintings of Cézanne's early period.

Cézanne later said. His friend and mentor was nine years older than he was, and was a firm believer in Cézanne's exceptional talent.

The first thing Pissarro did was to encourage him to banish dark colours from his palette. He himself had removed black, ochre and sienna from the range of colours he used. "Only paint with the three primary colours (red, yellow, blue) and their derivatives," he advised Cézanne. He showed him how to build up a picture from light-dark contrasts and, most importantly, encouraged him to observe nature conscientiously, transferring onto canvas only what he saw, without interpreting it or adding anything from his own imagination. He believed that the artist should be nothing more than an alert, conscientious observer of reality.

Pissarro also advised Cézanne not to use lines to outline the forms of his motifs. Rather, objects should be built up by gradations of tonal value.

"Do not work bit by bit," he advised Cézanne, "apply colour everywhere and observe the tonal values closely in relation to the surroundings. Paint with small brushstrokes and try to record your observations immediately. The eye must not concentrate on a specific point, but should absorb everything and in doing so note the reflections of colours on their surroundings. Work on the sky, the water, the branches and the earth simultaneously, and keep on improving what you do until the whole thing works. Cover the whole canvas in the first sitting, and work until there is nothing more to add. Observe the aerial perspective closely from the foreground to the horizon, the reflection of the sky and the foliage.

Do not be afraid of applying strong colour; gradually refine your work. Do not follow rules and principles, but paint what you see and feel. Paint boldly and without hesitation, because it is important to get your first impressions down. And do not be shy of nature! You must be bold, even at the risk of going wrong and making mistakes. There is only one teacher: nature…"

The two friends often chose the same subjects, painting side by side. "We were always together," Pissarro reported later, "but each of us kept the only thing which matters: our own perceptions."

Landscape, 1870/71
Oil on canvas, 53.7 x 65 cm (21¼ x 25½ in.)
Frankfurt/Main, Städel Museum

Unlike *Snow Thaw in L'Estaque*, Cézanne has used an unspectacular natural formation as his motif: a forest path on a rocky pine-covered hillside. However, the contrasting colours and interplay of light and shade make this simple subject very expressive, and its effect is due to the fact that Cézanne has painted reality as he sees it, without embellishment.

Édouard Manet
Olympia, 1863
Oil on canvas, 130 x 190 cm (51¼ x 74¾ in.)
Paris, Musée d'Orsay

Édouard Manet
Le déjeuner sur l'herbe, 1863
Oil on canvas, 208 x 264 cm (82 x 104 in.)
Paris, Musée d'Orsay

PAGE 25
The House of Dr Gachet in Auvers, c. 1873
Oil on canvas, 46 x 38 cm (18 x 15 in.)
Paris, Musée d'Orsay

From late 1872 to the spring of 1874, Cézanne
lived in Dr Paul Gachet's house in Auvers-
sur-Oise. Gachet was the first person to buy
pictures from him.

Cézanne even went so far as to make a faithful copy of a painting by
Pissarro to familiarize himself with his friend's technique. He did not always
find it easy to paint short, patient brushstrokes side by side on the canvas.
But he felt that Impressionist techniques brought him nearer to his aim and
helped rein in his wayward temperament. Cézanne's short, relaxed and free
brushstrokes, resembling those of the Impressionists, gradually became
more even and angular, often painted in parallel diagonals. The spots
of paint which he so energetically applied to the canvas had strong
shapes which give his pictures a rigorous, serious effect. The impression of
flamboyant haste was replaced by a feeling of stability and permanence.

Cézanne continued to work quietly at Pissarro's side. He made progress,
and Pissarro thought very highly of him. "Our friend, Cézanne, raises our
expectations," he reported, "and I have seen and have at home a painting of
remarkable vigour and power. If, as I hope, he stays some time in Auvers,
where he is going to live, he will astonish a lot of artists who were too hasty
in condemning him."

Another admirer of his paintings, Dr Paul-Fernand Gachet, had come to
live in Auvers-sur-Oise, a neighbouring village to Pontoise. Dr Gachet was
a highly distinctive character with unorthodox views, who dyed his hair
yellow and wore unconventional clothes. He admired Gustave Courbet and
Victor Hugo and frequented the Paris cafés where avant-garde artists met.
He also dabbled in painting in his spare time and was interested in everything which was new and revolutionary. He had met Cézanne through
Pissarro, and he persuaded him to come and live nearby in Auvers.

There, amid the total tranquility of the idyllic countryside, Cézanne
discovered the many subtle nuances of nature. He constantly overpainted
and corrected his paintings to preserve the rich sumptuousness of the reality
he observed. He was never satisfied, and never really felt he had completed
a painting. He would keep bringing out the canvas again and again and try
to record what he had seen in even greater detail.

He felt happy in the company of Gachet and his wife; for the first time,
someone was displaying a passionate interest in his work.

One day, the discussion turned to Manet's painting *Olympia* (1863, ill.
p. 24), the work which had caused such a scandal at the Salon of 1863, and
Cézanne's version, *A Modern Olympia*, painted three years previously
(1869/70, ill. p. 31). Cézanne promptly took up his brush and painted a second version, unusually quickly by his standards (1873/74, ill. p. 32). This
relaxed painting, full of subtle irony, differs from the earlier version, which
was stiffer and clumsier; it has a soft, delicate vividness which captures the
sensuality of the scene. The unadorned, direct realism of the naked prostitute, who appears to the customer as though in a haze of opium, as the un-
attainable object of his desire, is completely different from the very cool,
distancing view of nudity in Manet's *Olympia*.

However, there are parallels with Cézanne's painting *Déjeuner sur l'herbe*
(1869/70, ill. p. 30). In both figures, the artist himself is shown with his back
to us, in the same pose and wearing the same clothes, right down to the

PAGE 26
The House of Père Lacroix in Auvers, 1873
Oil on canvas, 61.3 x 50.6 cm (24¼ x 20 in.)
Washington, D.C., National Gallery of Art,
Collection Chester Dale

Although Cézanne's paintings from this
period are brighter and more vibrant than
his early works, they are more strictly
composed than those of the Impressionists
who, like him, came to Auvers to paint.

PAGE 27
View of Auvers-sur-Oise – The Fence, c. 1873
Oil on canvas, 44.5 x 34.5 cm (17½ x 13½ in.)
Private collection

Cézanne's palette became much brighter
as a result of working with Pissarro. He increasingly avoided continuous areas of
dark colour in favour of a more relaxed,
dotted style of painting.

black top hat. Both times, temptation lies in front of him on a white cloth:
in *Déjeuner sur l'herbe* it takes the form of apples, the "forbidden fruits"; in
A Modern Olympia it is an unreal dreamlike image, transcending the banal
reality of everyday life. Dr Gachet bought this second version of 1873 (ill.
p. 32). It was the first time Cézanne had sold one of his paintings.

Cézanne continued to express his visions of the female in paintings, in
an attempt to come to terms with his obsessions and fears. But the older he
grew, the more he avoided contact with women, and it was not long before
his feelings for Hortense Fiquet were a thing of the past. Closest to him were
his mother and his sister Marie, whom he greatly loved. Later, when he was
living mainly in Aix, he stopped using female models altogether, partly out
of consideration for the prudish, provincial attitudes of the local people, but
partly also because throughout his life he never managed to rid himself of
his shyness, fear and mistrust of women.

In 1873, again through Pissarro, Cézanne met the Parisian paint dealer
Julien Tanguy, a Breton aged about fifty, who immediately struck up a strong
rapport with him. "Père Tanguy" had strong opinions about art and sup-
ported Pissarro, Sisley, Van Gogh (whom Cézanne met at his house),
Guillaumin, Gauguin, Signac and Seurat by accepting paintings in exchange
for supplies of canvas and paint. Meeting Tanguy was a great stroke of luck
for Cézanne: Tanguy acquired many of his paintings and at least freed him
from the worry of obtaining materials. Nonetheless, Cézanne's financial situation was worse than it had ever been. He had a small bachelor's allowance
to feed a family of three, and he was far from achieving public recognition
or selling any paintings.

The other artists in the Batignolles group were faring no better. Their
paintings were still being rejected by the jury at the Salon, whose criteria
had not changed under the Third Republic. Only Manet's Old Master-like
painting *Le bon bock* was accepted by the Salon in 1873.

The young painters realized that they had no chance of getting into the
official Salon, and so they returned to Monet's plan, hatched in the Café
Guerbois back in 1867, to organize and finance their own group exhibition.

The exhibition by the Société anonyme des artistes, peintres, sculpteurs,
graveurs etc., as the group was officially called, was held in the studio of the
photographer Gaspard Félix Nadar on the Boulevard des Capucines. It
opened on 15 April 1874 and lasted for a month. The exhibition included
works by Renoir, Monet, Sisley, Berthe Morisot, Degas and Pissarro, as well
as by some less controversial artist friends of Degas. Pissarro invited
Cézanne to exhibit, against the wishes of some of the members, who feared
that Cézanne's very daring paintings could damage the group. Manet
promptly and angrily withdrew from the exhibition, describing Cézanne
as "a bricklayer who paints with his trowel." He hoped to achieve greater
success by taking part in the official Salon.

The exhibition unleashed a hail of ridicule and hilarity among the public
and the critics. They joked that the artists must have painted their pictures
by loading pistols with tubes of paint and firing them at their canvases.

Cézanne, as the painter of *A Modern Olympia*, was described by the critic of *L'Artiste* as a madman painting in a state of *delirium tremens*. Zola, who as a friend could have taken up the cudgels on the group's behalf, was not forthcoming. He was more interested in his gigantic series of novels, the family epic *Les Rougon-Macquart*. He visited the exhibition, but only to take notes for his novel about an artist, *L'Œuvre*, whose hero was reputedly Cézanne.

The novel describes the Batignolles group exhibition as follows:

"These laughs were no longer smothered by the handkerchiefs of the ladies, and the men distended their bellies the better to give vent to them. It was the contagious mirth of a crowd that had come for entertainment, was becoming excited by degrees, exploded apropos of nothing, and was enlivened as much by beautiful things as by execrable ones… every canvas had its appreciation, people called one another over to point out a good one, witty remarks were constantly being passed from mouth to mouth… The round and stupid mouth of the ignorant who criticize painting, expressing

The House of the Hanged Man at Auvers, 1873
Oil on canvas, 55 x 66 cm (21¾ x 26 in.)
Paris, Musée d'Orsay

The first exhibition by the Impressionists (the name was coined by a critic based on Monet's painting *Impression – Sunrise*) on 15 April 1874 met with public ridicule and incomprehension. Visitors came in droves, but only to mock. This was one of the few paintings which was sold during the exhibition; it was bought by the Count of Doria for 300 francs.

Déjeuner sur l'herbe, 1869/70
Oil on canvas, 60 x 80 cm (23½ x 31½ in.)
Private collection

Manet's motif of the *Déjeuner sur l'herbe* is taken up in a very distinctive and dramatic composition by Cézanne. Unlike in Manet's painting, it is difficult to identify the relationships between the figures here, though the figure in the foreground with his back to us is probably the artist himself. The apples, as symbolic objects, form the focal point of the composition.

the sum total of asininity, of absurd commentary, of bad and stupid ridicule, that an original work can evoke from bourgeois imbecility."

A critic from the satirical magazine *Charivari* scornfully dubbed the group the "Impressionists," after Monet's painting, *Impression – Sunrise*. This name quickly caught on, and replaced the original tag, "Intransigeants."

The mercilessly scathing verdict from the critics inevitably helped to deter potential buyers. But some paintings were sold, including Cézanne's work *The House of the Hanged Man at Auvers* (1873, ill. p. 29), which was bought by a collector, the Count of Doria, for 300 francs.

When the final accounts were drawn up for the exhibition, there was a deficit of 184.50 francs for each participant. Cézanne probably had to ask his father to settle his debts, and in May 1874 he went back to his parents' house in Aix-en-Provence.

Although the enterprise had been a failure of the first order, Cézanne remained self-confident, and seemed to be increasingly indifferent to public opinion. Back in Paris, he wrote to his mother:

"I begin to find myself superior to those around me, and you know that the good opinion I have of myself has only been reached after mature

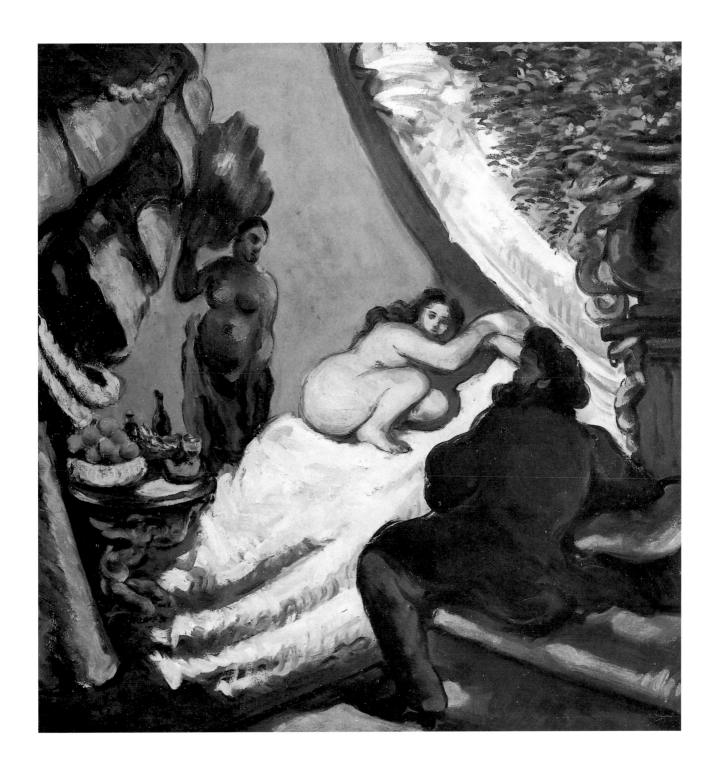

A Modern Olympia, 1869/70
Oil on canvas, 57.5 x 57 cm (22¾ x 22½ in.)
Private collection

Inspired by Manet's scandalous painting of 1863,
Cézanne painted a wildly expressive version
of the motif.

A Modern Olympia, 1873/74
Oil on canvas, 46 x 55 cm (18 x 21¾ in.)
Paris, Musée d'Orsay

*"On Sunday the public saw fit to sneer at a fantastic figure that is revealed
under an opium sky to a drug addict. This apparition of pink and nude
flesh pushed, in the empyrean cloud, by a kind of demon or incubus, like
a voluptuous vision – this corner of artificial paradise, has left even the
most courageous gasping for breath. Mr Cézanne merely gives the impression
of being a sort of madman who paints in delirium tremens."*

— THIS WAS A FEMALE CRITIC'S OPINION OF CÉZANNE'S PAINTING
AT THE FIRST IMPRESSIONIST EXHIBITION IN APRIL 1874.

Afternoon in Naples (Rum Punch), *c.* 1875
Oil on canvas, 37 x 45 cm (14½ x 17¾ in.)
Canberra, National Gallery of Australia

This openly provocative and sensual painting
shows a naked couple in bed, being served with
a love potion by an exotic serving-maid. The
picture was regarded as an offence against public decency, as well as against the Salon, and of
course this unambiguous painting was rejected.

consideration. I must always work, but not to achieve a final polish, which is for the admiration of imbeciles. And this thing which is commonly so appreciated is only the accomplishment of an artisan's skill and makes every work resulting from it inartistic and vulgar. I must strive after completion only for the pleasure of giving added truth and learning. And believe me, there always comes a time when one arrives, and one has much more fervent and devoted admirers than those who are flattered by vain appearances."

Because of the artists' desperate financial straits, there was no question of organizing a group exhibition in 1875. Instead, they held an auction of their paintings in the Hôtel Drouot. This was a fiasco, and a financial disaster, but it did bring them into contact with an enthusiastic art-lover and collector, a customs inspector named Victor Chocquet. Through Renoir, Chocquet soon met Cézanne, and a warm and close friendship grew up between the two.

Chocquet was the quintessential private collector who follows only his own tastes and ignores passing fashions and public opinion. His friendship

Pool at the Jas de Bouffan, c. 1878/79
Oil on canvas, 92 x 80 cm (36¼ x 31½ in.)
Buffalo, New York, Albright-Knox Art Gallery,
Fellows for Life Fund, 1927

The grounds of the Jas de Bouffan, with their avenue of chestnut trees and stone pool, were the subject of many of Cézanne's paintings. The bright colours and parallel layers of brushstrokes reflect the influence of Pissarro.

with Cézanne was strengthened by the fact that both of them revered Eugène Delacroix.

Chocquet had accumulated a significant collection of paintings and antiques in his apartment in the Rue de Rivoli, including twenty works by Delacroix alone, and works by Courbet, Manet and Corot. When the Impressionists held their second exhibition in 1876, he loaned paintings by Renoir, Pissarro and Monet.

Cézanne did not take part in this second exhibition, possibly because he could not afford to pay his share of the cost. He submitted one painting to the Salon which, as always, was rejected. At the beginning of April, when the exhibition opened, he was already back in Provence.

Increasingly he became aware that the Provençal landscape came closest to his artistic objectives. Its bright light and strong contrasts, its parched, barren appearance and sharply defined forms were in complete contrast to the gentle, undulating landscapes of the Île-de-France painted by his Impressionist friends. The Aix region was also rich in natural formations, with its jagged cliffs and cracked earth providing powerful contrasts.

The light there was not the soft, dispersed light which gives the countryside a gentle, cheerful appearance. The sun was merciless, the light

Trees in the Jas de Bouffan, 1875/76
Oil on canvas, 54 x 73 cm (21¼ x 28¾ in.)
Private collection

The motif in itself is unspectacular, but Cézanne has made intensive but carefully controlled use of colour to create a sundrenched park landscape.

The Eternal Feminine, *c.* 1877
Oil on canvas, 43.2 x 53.3 cm (17 x 21 in.)
Malibu, The J. Paul Getty Museum

A broad cross-section of male society pays
homage to its naked idol, who is holding court
under a white canopy in a room which looks
out over the countryside. The female figure
has been stripped of her individuality, and
lies defenceless and exposed to the men's gaze;
she is subject and object, exploiter and exploited
all in one. This painting bears witness to
Cézanne's own mixture of fear and longing
for the female sex.

glittering and harsh, and any clouds were whisked away by the Mistral to leave a steely blue sky.

In this landscape Cézanne found the basic, unchanging structures of nature, which vary little from one hour to the next or from season to season.

The wiry vegetation, and the evergreen foliage of the olive trees, pines, cypresses and oaks, suited his slow pace of working; even if he spent months working on a landscape, it changed very little. This meant that he could re-construct nature on the canvas, as he perceived it, in complete tranquillity and with rigorous discipline.

In the summer, he went to L'Estaque, which was then an idyllic fishing village on a bay in the Mediterranean, to paint landscapes for Victor Chocquet. Around six years had elapsed between *Snow Thaw in L'Estaque*

The Temptation of St Anthony, c. 1877
Oil on canvas, 47.2 x 56 cm (18½ x 22 in.)
Paris, Musée d'Orsay

The legend of St Anthony, the Egyptian hermit, was a particularly popular subject with artists in the second half of the 19th century. Cézanne has transposed the "temptation" to a romantic level and particularly emphasizes the sexual aspect of the story.

The Sea at L'Estaque, 1876
Oil on canvas, 42 x 59 cm (16½ x 23¼ in.)
Zurich, Fondation Rau pour le Tiers-Monde

"It is like a playing-card. Red roofs on the blue sea… The sun is so terrifying that it seems as though the objects are silhouetted, not only in black or white, but also in blue, red, brown, and violet." (Paul Cézanne, 1876)

(*c.* 1870, ill. p. 22) and *The Sea at L'Estaque* (1876, ill. p. 38) – and what a change! Cézanne had clearly learned a great deal from Pissarro during this period, and added a great deal of his own. This brightly coloured seascape is serene and formal. The painting is carefully structured, with the strong colours – the terracotta roof tiles, the green foliage, the blue surface of the water – covering the surface of the canvas with an even intensity. There is no definable lighting; only the red chimney is glowing in the low sun.

It is not the light which breaks up the outlines of the forms and renders them hazy and indeterminate, and this has a very disorienting effect. Instead of light, the forms are defined by strength and modulation of colour. It is colour which determines the nature of objects and both brings them nearer to the viewer and places them an immeasurable distance away. We can see from this painting that Cézanne has become a close observer of nature, and nothing has been added purely for effect. Of course the artist's particular viewpoint has been carefully chosen, and the diagonals of the hill and the overlapping tree trunks have been deliberately included to create tension. But this picture is one of mature tranquility, showing the artist's profound respect for the splendour of the landscape.

On 2 July 1876, Cézanne wrote to Pissarro about L'Estaque:

"I have not been in Aix for the past month. I have begun two small pictures of the sea for Mr Chocquet, who had spoken to me about them. It is like a playing-card. Red roofs on the blue sea. If the weather gets better, I could possibly finish them both. As things are at the moment, I have not done anything yet. But there are compositions which would take three to four months' work, which could probably be done, because the vegetation does not change. There are olive trees and stone pines, which always keep their leaves. The sun is so terrifying that it seems as though the objects are silhouetted, not only in black or white, but also in blue, red, brown, and violet. I may be mistaken, but it seems to me to be the very opposite of modelling. How happy our gentle landscape painters from Auvers would be here… If I can, I will spend at least a month in this place, for one would need to paint pictures at least two metres in size."

Roofs, c. 1877
Oil on canvas, 47 x 59 cm (18½ x 23¼ in.)
Private collection

This is one of Cézanne's few townscapes, painted in bright, Impressionist colours and flowing brushstrokes by the "Little Master of Impressionism," as he once described himself.

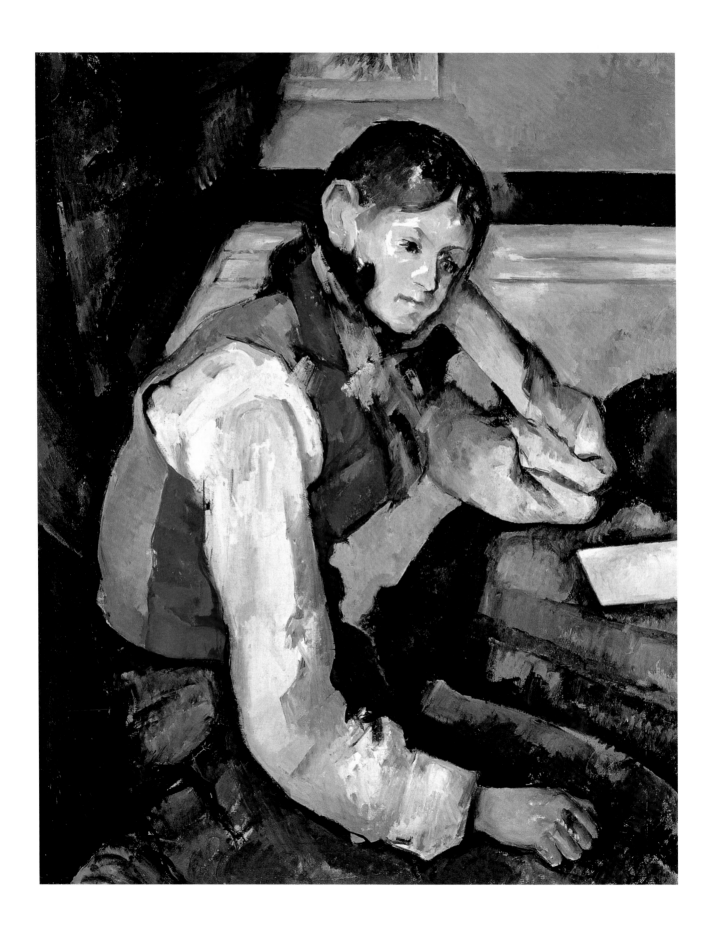

"Harmony in Parallel with Nature"

"The artist who has been the most attacked, the most mistreated by the press and the public for the past fifteen years is Mr Cézanne. There is no outrageous epithet that has not been attached to his name; his books have had a success in ridicule and continue to have it… For my part, I do not know of any painting less laughable than this."

Georges Rivière, an art critic and friend of Renoir, wrote a defence of Cézanne during the Impressionists' third group exhibition, in May 1877. He continued:

"Mr Cézanne is, in his works, a Greek of the great period; his canvases have the calm and heroic serenity of the paintings and terracottas of antiquity… His beautiful still lifes, so exact in the relationship of tones, have a solemn quality of truth. In all his paintings, the artist produces emotion because he himself experiences violent emotion in the face of nature that all his craftsmanship transmits to the canvas."

But Georges Rivière's was a lone voice; few showed such sympathy and understanding for Cézanne's new and subjective approach to painting after seeing the exhibition. The comments in the Paris newspapers, which gave detailed coverage to events in the art world, were largely mocking and cynical. Cézanne decided to stop exhibiting with the Impressionists (although they asked him not to leave), and to concentrate more on getting into the Salon.

Towards the end of the year he returned to southern France to paint in L'Estaque. The paintings from this period include two landscapes showing Cézanne's view of nature in two very different ways. In *Rocks at L'Estaque* (1882–85, ill. p. 44), Cézanne is particularly interested in the rocky pinnacles, scarred by erosion and covered in sparse, wiry vegetation, but he gives us nothing by which we can gauge the actual size of this natural formation. Are the rocks so huge that a person standing in the foreground would have been dwarfed by them, or are we looking at them close-up, so that they are in fact fairly small? There is no way of knowing, and the roof near the sea, the only sign of civilization in this vast natural landscape, does not help to establish a sense of scale. The proportions remain unclear.

PAGE 42
Boy in a Red Waistcoat, c. 1888–90
Oil on canvas, 79.5 x 64 cm (31¼ x 25¼ in.)
Zurich, Stiftung Sammlung E. G. Bührle

This painting, whose tension derives wholly from the distribution of areas of colour, was described by Gustave Geffroy as a work which "bears comparison with the finest figure pictures in painting."

Cézanne has used a very limited palette in this painting: bluish-grey for the rocks, green for the vegetation, and ochre for the soil; but there are complex tonalities within this small range of colours. The rocks on the left of the picture are lit by the late evening sun and are painted in light ochre, while the overhangs of the rocks are in shadow and are painted a dark, saturated blackish-green. Very subtle nuances of colour in the foreground are used to create the dramatic effect of the setting sun, while the background of sea and hills is uniform and monochrome in structure.

But the dramatic appearance of the rock formations is not primarily the result of a momentary effect of light, or where the sun happens to be at that particular moment. Rather, the light seems to come from the objects themselves. The effects of colour and form reinforce each other, breaking down the landscape into a huge agglomeration of spots of colour.

Here again, Cézanne has used the technique of short brushstrokes which he learned from Pissarro. But he has used it with great freedom; where he wants to create compact forms whose structure is defined by light, he uses larger, more solid brushstrokes, whereas the areas of vegetation, which have a greater variety of colour, are created using smaller, more broken strokes.

Cézanne used a more traditional composition in his painting *The Sea at L'Estaque* (1878/79, ill. p. 45), which was acquired by Pablo Picasso in the 1940s. The eye is led from the road running across the picture in the foreground to the village on the hillside and finally to the sea, which stretches to the horizon in the far distance. This horizontal structure is broken by the vertical chimney and the two trees in the foreground, which, very much in the Baroque tradition of the *repoussoir* or strong foreground, increase the feeling of depth in the painting. Here we can clearly see the artistic problems

Rocks at L'Estaque, 1882–85
Oil on canvas, 73 x 91 cm (28¾ x 36 in.)
Museu de Arte de São Paulo,
Assis Chateaubriand

The Sea at L'Estaque, 1878/79
Oil on canvas, 73 x 92 cm (28¾ x 36¼ in.)
Paris, Musée Picasso

*Cézanne has clearly separated the planes of the
picture and used the Baroque tradition of the
repoussoir to increase the impression of depth.*

of linking the planes together, the treatment of the large area of sea, and the
conflict between line and plane.

Life in L'Estaque caused Cézanne considerable difficulties. He had
installed Hortense and their son Paul in a small apartment and travelled
back and forth between L'Estaque and Aix, constantly fearing that his
father might discover the existence of his family.

Louis-Auguste Cézanne had retired from his banking business after the
Franco-Prussian War. He transferred his assets to his two daughters and his
son Paul to reduce their liability to inheritance tax.

This did not mean that they could actually make use of the money; it was
administered by their father, who was more distrustful of Paul than ever
before: his son had disappointed him in every respect. He found out about
Cézanne's liaison when Victor Chocquet inadvertently let slip a comment
about "Madame Cézanne and little Paul," and promptly reduced his monthly
allowance by half. Cézanne was forced to ask his friend Zola for help.

Although Cézanne still occasionally went out painting from nature with
Pissarro, he was becoming increasingly distant from the Impressionists. He

felt that Impressionist paintings were too transient, too much rooted in the moment. Cézanne was not satisfied simply with putting down what he saw onto canvas; he wanted to penetrate deep into the heart of nature and depict what was immutable and permanent in it. "You must think," he wrote; "the eye is not enough, it needs to think as well."

Cézanne would work on the same painting for long periods, sometimes months at a time. Transient, momentary effects of light and reflections were of secondary importance; indeed, they were almost a hindrance. "Nature causes me the greatest of difficulties," he wrote to Zola in 1879. He would sit with stubborn determination in front of his subject, contemplating nature and trying to understand the essence of things: their inherent, eternal form. His goal as an artist was to give things permanence. This meant that every subject had to be placed in a compositional balance which was the result of calculation, reflection and logic.

The same carefully structured compositions are apparent in his portraits. His *Madame Cézanne in Blue* (*c.* 1888–90, ill. p. 53) shows Hortense sitting against a background which is divided into two parts: on the right is a door, with strictly geometrical panelling; on the left is patterned wallpaper and the ornamental top of an occasional table. The pale, cool blue of the door is in sharp contrast with the warm earthy tones of the wall-hanging and the piece of furniture. Hortense is posed leaning slightly to one side, a motionless, monumental figure. The flesh tints of her serious, withdrawn-looking face echo the colours of the background, and the opening of her jacket also helps to divide the composition into two. The formal severity of the composition, which is built up using colours, and its concentration on the essentials, create an unbridgeable distance between ourselves and the subject of the portrait.

Chestnut Trees at the Jas de Bouffan in Winter,
c. 1885/86
Oil on canvas, 73 x 92 cm (28¾ x 36¼ in.)
Minneapolis Institute of Arts,
The William Hood Dunwoody Fund

Cézanne may faithfully depict what he sees, but he orders nature to fit his own compositional rules; the chestnut trees are arranged more neatly in the painting than they are in real life.

The expressionless, inward-looking gaze creates a sense of timelessness, but without depriving the subject of her individuality. Cézanne uses a similar process in his portraits to that of his landscapes: they are formal, strict, with a monumental, permanent quality.

Cézanne was still dissatisfied with the results of his work, and even showed some sympathy with the jury of the Salon when they turned down yet another of his paintings. "I understand very well that it could not be accepted, because of my point of departure, which was too far away from the objective to be achieved, namely the reproduction of nature." This reproduction of nature took place in two stages in Cézanne's work. Before he actually began painting, he would spend a long time looking at the subject. Cézanne had to "read" the subject first, and understand its essence, before he could start painting. Then, in the second stage, he would "realize" the structure of the painting based on the forms, colours and structures which he had created in this preliminary image. In this process, it was important that such forms were taken from the natural world and not from the painter's own

House and Farm at Jas de Bouffan, 1885–87
Oil on canvas, 60 x 71 cm (23½ x 28 in.)
Prague, Národnígalerie

The Jas de Bouffan estate provided an unfailing source of peace and tranquility for Cézanne. In this picture, the house seems to be drawing the sun into itself, almost turning to face it.

Studies, *c.* 1883
Pencil and black chalk, 48.5 x 32 cm
(19 x 12½ in.)
Rotterdam, Museum Boijmans Van Beuningen

This page contains sketches spanning several
years: a "Lament of Psyche" from the Louvre,
a self-portrait, aged about forty-five, and
a portrait of the artist's young son asleep.

imagination. The forms must retain a similarity with nature; they must
remain "true" to it. Cézanne's need to be true to nature did not simply mean
reproducing exactly what he saw; nor did it mean superficial imitation. "We
should not be satisfied with strict reality," Émile Bernard quotes him as say-
ing, "the reforming process which a painter carries out as a result of his own
personal way of seeing things gives a new interest to the depiction of nature.
As a painter, he is revealing something which no-one has ever seen before
and translating it into the absolute concepts of painting. That is, into something other than reality." These "absolute concepts of painting" are colours
and forms, and the spatial relationships between them. Cézanne believed that
being true to nature meant being true to these relationships. So he sought to
create a new harmony, which he called "harmony in parallel with nature."

Around the middle of the 1880s, Cézanne painted *House and Farm at Jas
de Bouffan* (1885–87, ill. p. 47), an unusual picture of his father's house in Aix.
This house represented a haven of tranquillity amid all the difficulties of
Cézanne's life. What is unusual about this particular painting, of a subject
which he depicted many times, is the fact that the house has a distinct tilt to
the left. The greyish-green hill on the right is also tilted in this same diagonal
axis, as are the sunlit sides of the smaller outbuildings on the right. These are
similar in colour to the yellow-orange tones of the main house, but slightly
lighter, creating a diagonal tension which is accentuated by the bright red
angular roof. The deep green of the embankment also provides a counter-
point to the red roof of the house. There is therefore a contrast of colour between the complementary reds and greens, and a contrast of form between
the linearity of the roof and the organic, rounded form of the embankment.
The bright green of the strip of grass at the bottom left is also just visible in
the greenish-blue of the sky at the top left. This painting therefore contains
two overlapping contrasts; these are not static, but are given movement by
the fact that the house is inclined slightly backwards.

What were the feelings of the painter, what were his personal perceptions
of the Jas de Bouffan, the "House of the Wind," when he painted this oddly
angled picture of it? Like a person deliberately facing the sun to soak up as
many of its warming rays as possible, the Jas de Bouffan is tilted slightly backwards so that its full richness of colour is revealed. The brightest area of blue
in the picture is not the sky, but the open shutters, drawing the warmth of a
Provençal summer's day into the house and turning it into a three-dimensional space. It comes as something of a surprise that although the planes of
the painting are fairly compressed, and the house has a flat façade, it is actually
a solid body. This impression could have been created using a strong source
of sunlight from a particular angle, but it is not. The whole of the picture
seems suffused with sunshine. The light comes from the colours themselves.

"We must not paint what we think we see, but what we see," Cézanne told
the young poet Jean Royère in the mid-1890s. "Sometimes it may go against
the grain, but this is what our craft demands… People will teach you the laws
of perspective at the Beaux-Arts, but they have never seen that depth results
from a juxtaposition of vertical and horizontal surfaces, and that is what

perspective is. I have discovered it after long efforts, and I have painted in surfaces, because I do nothing which I have not seen, and what I paint exists."

So Cézanne's concern was far from being that of conveying the illusion of a three-dimensional world to the viewer. Rather he was creating a new reality using the two-dimensional surface of the painting. He simply sought to create an awareness of the two-dimensionality of the picture, this new "realization" of nature, and so it was important for him to avoid using traditional linear perspective, which creates the illusion of three-dimensional depth. In addition, if he had used strict linear perspective, he would have had to depict every object the size required by perspective. But what Cézanne wanted to do was to show each object the size which he saw it. Apart from rejecting linear perspective, Cézanne also steered clear of the superior perspective so beloved of the Impressionists, in which the colours and forms of objects become more vague and indistinct the farther they are from the viewer.

Cézanne believed that colours and forms should be given equal weight and clarity wherever they appeared in the picture. The surface of the painting

The Château de Médan, 1879–81
Oil on canvas, 59 x 72 cm (23¼ x 28¼ in.)
Glasgow, Kelvingrove Art Gallery and Museum

Cézanne used his visits to Zola's summer house in Médan to paint in the open air in the surrounding area, including Auvers, Pontoise and Bennecourt.

PAGE 51
Mardi Gras, 1888
Oil on canvas, 100 x 81 cm (39¼ x 32 in.)
Moscow, Pushkin Museum

Cézanne's son Paul, and Paul's friend Louis
Guillaume, posed for these figures from the
Italian Commedia dell'arte, an unusual motif
for the artist. Louis reportedly fainted during
one sitting because Cézanne insisted that he
should not move.

should be uniform in structure, and should eschew any form of illusion or
naturalism. This meant that the incidence of light had to be almost the same
throughout the picture, and he therefore largely avoided any references to a
recognizable light source and the use of heavy shadows. The light is even,
and comes from within the painting itself; the objects radiate their own light.

So if Cézanne avoided using traditional methods of creating space, how
did he manage to ensure that his paintings nevertheless suggest space, without destroying the unity of the surface? He made use of the knowledge that
cold colours, such as blue and green, appear to recede, and warm colours –
red, orange, yellow – seem to stand out from the surface. He used this effect
in his painting *Mardi Gras* (1888, ill. p. 51). Another method which Cézanne
used to create depth was the use of overlapping forms. This combination of
flatness and depth is particularly conspicuous in his paintings of Mont
Sainte-Victoire. "I try to render perspective through colour alone," explained
Cézanne. "I proceed very slowly, for nature reveals herself to me in very complex form, and constant progress must be made. One must see one's model
correctly and experience it in the right way, and furthermore, express oneself
with distinction and strength."

In April 1886, Cézanne married Hortense Fiquet in Aix, in the presence of
his parents. After so long, he decided to make his relationship with Hortense
official, despite not having loved her for a long time, was probably to ensure
that Paul did not suffer the stigma of having unmarried parents. Six months
later, Cézanne's father died, aged eighty-eight, and Cézanne at last was able to
claim his inheritance. For the first time in his life, the 47-year-old painter was
financially independent. "My father was a man of genius," he said, looking
back. "He left me an income of 25,000 francs."

Study for Mardi Gras, 1886/87
Pencil, 24.5 x 30.6 cm (9¾ x 12 in.)
Private collection

PAGE 52
Self-Portrait with a Palette, c. 1890
Oil on canvas, 92 x 73 cm (36¼ x 28¾ in.)
Zurich, Stiftung Sammlung E. G. Bührle

TOP
Madame Cézanne in Blue, 1888–90
Oil on canvas, 74.1 x 61 cm (29¼ x 24 in.)
Houston, The Museum of Fine Arts,
The Robert Lee Blaffer Memorial Collection,
Gift of Sarah Campbell Blaffer

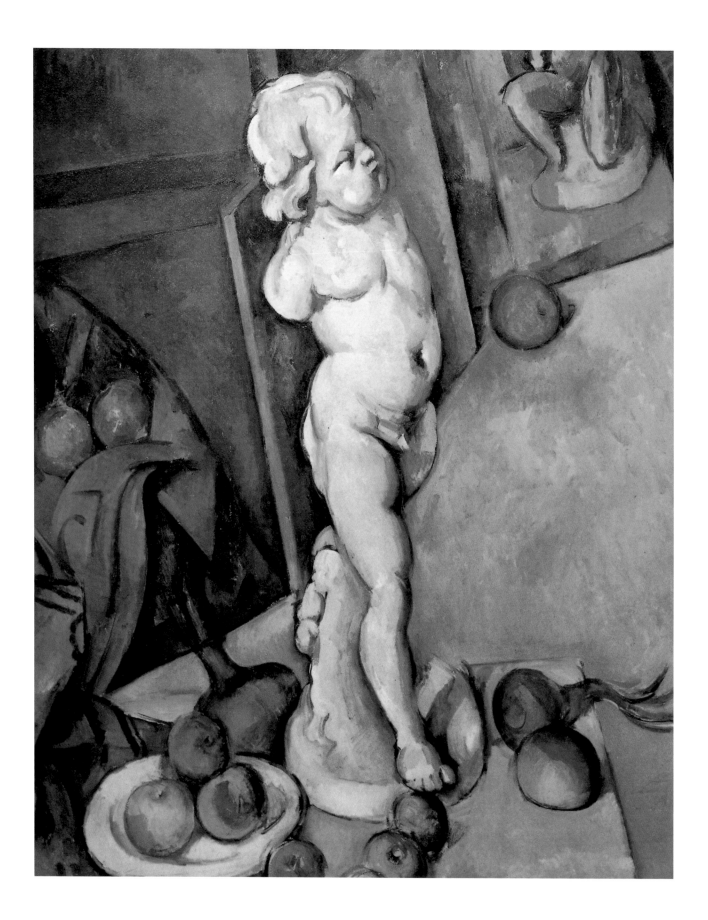

"I Should Like to Astonish Paris with an Apple" – The Still Lifes

Cézanne developed a completely new way of depicting objects in space. He reinvented still lifes on the basis of their two-dimensionality, and used purely artistic means to give them depth.

In *Cherries and Peaches* (1885–87, ill. p. 56), the plate of cherries is tilted conspicuously forwards, as though we were looking down on it from above. The same is true of the back part of the table, but the front of it is painted as though we are seeing it horizontally. The plate of peaches and the jug are also painted from a lower angle. There is a similar dual viewpoint in *Vessels, Basket and Fruit* (*The Kitchen Table*, 1888–90, ill. p. 57), but here the same object is shown from two different viewpoints; the top of the basket of fruit is shown from above, and the side is viewed from the front. Much the same happens with the ginger jar in his *Still Life* (1890–94, ill. p. 60). This is tilted forwards so that we can see in through the top, but the sides of the jar are depicted frontally. This distorted use of perspective suggests depth and at the same time emphasizes the two-dimensional nature of the picture's surface. As Cézanne avoided using linear perspective in his depictions of objects, he could paint them so that their size was in proportion to their importance in the composition as a whole.

In *Vessels, Baskets and Fruit*, for example, the pear on the right-hand edge of the table is disproportionately large. However, its size is important to the balance within the painting; it provides an offsetting counterpart to the variety of forms in the left-hand corner of the painting. Likewise, the red pear in the fold of the tablecloth, in the left foreground, counterbalances the similarly positioned red pear in the fruit basket. Although the forms in the painting appear at first sight to have been arranged at random, they in fact form a carefully thought-out composition which is full of tensions. Cézanne set up all his still lifes in the studio. Some of the objects he used are still in his last studio on the Chemin des Lauves in Aix (ill. p. 94 bottom). Apart from the fruit, many of the objects, such as jugs, pots and plates, frequently recur in his compositions. The pictures often include a dramatically billowing white tablecloth, giving the paintings a touch of Baroque extravagance.

Cherries and Peaches, 1885–87
Oil on canvas, 50.1 x 60.9 cm (19¾ x 24 in.)
Los Angeles County Museum of Art,
Gift of Adele R. Levy Fund, Inc., and
Mr. and Mrs. Armand S. Deutsch

The perspective of this picture is broken
in a number of ways; the plate of cherries is
shown from a different angle to the other
objects. The picture emphasizes the fact
that it is two-dimensional by refusing to
use any form of illusion.

The forms of the containers are simple and plain, and the fruits mainly
consist of very basic, round forms: onions, pears, peaches and large numbers
of apples. He found these fruits the easiest when it came to establishing volume; he did this using very subtle gradations of colour rather than resorting
to techniques such as outlining or shadows.

Although Cézanne arranged his still lifes very carefully, he took great
pains to avoid any impression of artificiality or sophisticated materiality; he
was not trying to create a perfect illusion. As a result, some of his still lifes
even show the normally unseen items, such as wooden blocks or books,
which he used to prop up objects in a tilted position.

The young artist Louis Le Bail wrote of these still-life arrangements by
Paul Cézanne: "The cloth was very slightly draped upon the table, with
innate taste. Then Cézanne arranged the fruits, contrasting the tones one
against the other, making the complementaries vibrate, the greens against
the reds, the yellows against the blues, tipping, turning, balancing the fruits
as he wanted them to be, using coins of one or two sous for the purpose.

Vessels, Basket and Fruit (The Kitchen Table),
1888–90
Oil on canvas, 65 x 81.5 cm (25½ x 32 in.)
Paris, Musée d'Orsay

What might seem like a random selection
of objects is in fact a balanced and carefully
thought-out composition. Each object is
painted the size which it needs to be to create
an equilibrium within the painting.

He brought to this task the greatest care and many precautions; one guessed
that it was a feast for the eye to him."

It was not the objects themselves that were meant to gain the viewer's
attention, but the arrangement of colours and forms on the surface, seen
through the artist's own eyes. This viewpoint, subjectively but deliberately
chosen and governed by the intellect, enabled Cézanne to create a new level
of reality on the canvas. He did not need elaborate objects and sumptuous
decoration to do this. On the contrary, the simplest objects were the best
when it came to realizing his concepts of depth, solidity and weight in a two-
dimensional structure. Clearly, compositions like these could not be painted
quickly. Cézanne built them up using individual small areas of paint spread
across the whole of the canvas, gradually developing these into the form and
volume of an object. These areas of paint were tonally balanced with one
another, or "modulated," and required a slow and careful style of working.
Cézanne would often spend endless amounts of time in front of the canvas
without painting a single brushstroke.

Basket of Apples, *c.* 1893 (detail)
Oil on canvas, 65 x 80 cm (25½ x 31½ in.)
Chicago, Art Institute, Helen Birch Bartlett
Memorial Collection

Still Life, 1890–94
Oil on canvas, 65.5 x 81.5 cm (25¾ x 32 in.)
Private collection

Émile Bernard, who recorded his memories of two visits to Cézanne in Aix, wrote of the artist's methods: "I gained an idea of the slowness of his work when he had installed me in his studio outside the town. While I worked on a still life which he had arranged for me in the downstairs room, I heard him moving back and forth in the upstairs studio. It was as though he was pacing across the room, thinking. He would keep coming downstairs, going into the garden, sitting down and then suddenly rushing back up to the studio. I often surprised him in the garden looking disheartened. He said to me then that I was something of a hindrance to him in his work."

Cézanne constantly reworked his paintings, spending months or – with breaks – years on some of them. But if he found that he could not achieve exactly the balance of colour which he sought, he would simply abandon paintings where they stood, or even destroy the canvas in fury at himself and his lack of success. The older Cézanne grew, the more he retreated into the solitude of the Jas de Bouffan. "Isolation is what I am worthy of. At least then no-one can get me in his clutches."

His irritability also grew as the result of diabetes, which he had been suffering from since 1890. His complex, sensitive and shy personality made it increasingly difficult for his fellow-beings to get on with him. He would often reject well-meaning gestures from friends and admirers out of fear that they might get too close to him.

Numa Coste, his friend from his youth in Aix, wrote to Émile Zola in the early 1890s: "[Cézanne] is well and physically solid, but he has become timid and primitive and younger than ever. He lives at the Jas de Bouffan with his mother who, for that matter, is on bad terms with the Ball [Cézanne's wife Hortense], who in turn does not get on with her sisters-in-law, nor they among themselves. So Paul lives on one side, his wife lives on the other. And it is one of the most touching things I know to see this good fellow retain his childlike naiveté, forget the disappointments of the struggle, and obstinately continue, resigned and suffering, the pursuit of a work he cannot produce."

Cézanne had, for some time, been growing increasingly distant from Émile Zola, his closest friend in the early days in Aix and Paris. The warmth

Still Life with Apples and Peaches, c. 1905
Oil on canvas, 81 x 100.5 cm (32 x 39½ in.)
Washington, D.C., National Gallery of Art,
Gift of Eugene and Agnes E. Meyer

"The pears, peaches, apples and onions, the vases, bowls and bottles seemed, partly because of the slight displacements and crooked surfaces, like fairytale objects which are just about to come to life. And yet it is clearly the moment before the earthquake, as though these things are the last." (Peter Handke, *Die Lehre der Sainte-Victoire*) of their friendship had cooled considerably. The more comfortable lifestyle which Zola was at last beginning to enjoy as a writer, and his luxurious house in Médan, must have alienated Cézanne, who was still leading a modest and unassuming existence. Cézanne visited Zola many times, often spending several weeks in Médan. But the final break between the two friends came in March 1886 with the publication of Zola's novel, *L'Œuvre*. The novel's protagonist, Claude Lantier, is an artist who fails to realize his ambitions and eventually commits suicide; he bears many resemblances to Cézanne.

The artist's pride must have been considerably wounded. His letter to Zola thanking him for sending a copy of the novel is very formal, distant and polite: "My dear Émile, I have just received *L'Œuvre*, which you were good enough to send me. I thank the author of *Les Rougon-Macquart* for this kind token of remembrance and ask him to permit me to clasp his hand while thinking of bygone years. Ever yours under the impulse of past times. Paul Cézanne."

The Card Players, 1890–95
Oil on canvas, 47.5 x 57 cm (18¾ x 22½ in.)
Paris, Musée d'Orsay

This was the last letter in the long correspondence between Paul Cézanne and Émile Zola.

In the 1890s, Cézanne continued to paint landscapes in and around the Jas de Bouffan, as well as still lifes and portraits. He often painted portraits of himself – his most patient model! For others, the endless sittings were often torture. Cézanne demanded that his models remain absolutely motionless, posing almost as though they were objects in his still lifes. To him, a head was no different from an apple as the basis for a composition; for Cézanne was not interested in the emotions or individual personalities of any of the people whose portraits he painted. For this reason, he tended to paint the kind of people whom he could afford to pay as models, such as the farmers and day labourers on the tenanted fields of the Jas de Bouffan. It was people like those who were used as the models for *The Card Players* (1890–92, ill. p. 63), of which he painted five different versions. He may have been led to use this motif by the anonymous painting of the same name in the Musée Granet in Aix.

The Card Players, 1890–92
Oil on canvas, 65.4 x 81.9 cm (25¾ x 32¼ in.)
New York, The Metropolitan Museum of Art,
Bequest of Stephen C. Clark, 1960

Cézanne wholly avoids any narrative, genrelike element which a motif of this kind could have contained and instead builds up a painting in accordance with strict rules of colour and form. This emphasizes the simple dignity of the ponderous Provençal day-labourers, who worked at the Jas de Bouffan and were paid to sit for Cézanne.

These compositions were based on detailed pencil, watercolour and oil studies. In successive paintings, the number of card players was gradually pared down to two, almost resembling a still life. Cézanne's *Card Players* are very far from being genre pieces, despite the fact that they show scenes from everyday life – the sturdy local peasant figures playing their beloved belote. Unlike the cheerful *joie de vivre* of Renoir's *Le Moulin de la Galette*, and more like Van Gogh's *The Potato-Eaters* of 1885, these paintings express the harsh melancholy of the Provençal countryside and its inhabitants. Their faces are serious, their shoulders seemingly weighed down by life's burdens. In the version with four card players, the cool, pale blue daylight is the dominant colour. The players' hands and faces are painted in a warm orange tone, suggesting concentration and inner tension amid all the external tranquility. This orange tone is taken up by the rumpled curtain in the top right-hand corner of the picture, with the motif of the pleated folds being extended down to the bottom edge of the picture by the right-hand player's peasant smock. The blue of the smock provides a cool contrast with the warm complementary orange of the curtain. The purpose of the curtain is purely compositional; it is not used to define the space as, say, a café outside Aix. Rather it helps to fix the composition in space, which is something the pastel blue wall does not do because of its lack of spatial determination. In addition, together with the pipe rack on the wall, the curtain creates a link with the standing onlooker as he concentrates on passively watching the game.

The composition used in the version of *The Card Players* with two players (1890–95, ill. p. 62) is very different. Here the background is mainly dark, and only a few light-coloured strips give an idea of the space, perhaps the roofed terrace of a café. The scene is lit by artificial light, which is reflected on the tablecloth, bottle and pipe. Here again, the purpose of the painting is not to recreate some everyday scene from small-town provincial life, but to solve the compositional problem of depicting people in space. The two men sit stiffly at the table, its edges receding into the background and culminating in the vertical axis with the bottle. The table is the centre of the scene; it is the meeting-point for the diagonals of the players' bent arms, as well as the focus of their gaze. The table is fully lit, and its warm orange tone provides a transition between the dull, cool bluish-grey of the left-hand player and the pale grey of the man on the right. Both the men's jackets contain echoes of the colour of the table.

Every detail in the painting serves a purpose and contributes to the overall effect. Nothing is left to chance. Far from painting a naturalistic or anecdotal scene, Cézanne has succeeded in creating a carefully thought-out composition of directional values and relationships between colours and forms. It is a monumental, and yet intimate scene.

PAGE 65
The Gardener, *c.* 1906
Oil on canvas, 65.4 x 54.9 cm (25¾ x 21½ in.)
London, Tate

65

The Painter and His Mountain –
Mont Sainte-Victoire

During the 1890s, Cézanne spent most of his time in Aix, though making frequent journeys to Paris. But the Provençal landscape had captivated him like no other. In the summer of 1896, which he spent in a health resort at Talloires on Lake Annecy, he wrote to his friend from his youth, Philippe Solari:

"When I was in Aix, it seemed to me that I should be better elsewhere; now that I am here, I miss Aix. Life for me is beginning to be of a sepulchral monotony… I paint to divert myself; it is not very amusing, but the lake is very nice with the big mountains all round… I have been told that they are two thousand metres high; it is not worth our country, though – without exaggeration – it is fine. But when one was born down there, it is no use, nothing else seems to mean anything."

Nevertheless, *Lake Annecy* (1896, ill. p. 68) is one of the most impressive of all the landscapes which Cézanne painted outside Provence. The surface of the water appears dense and impenetrable; its effect is motionless and tectonic, like that of the mountain which stands immediately behind it, a great, solid mass.

Cézanne constructed this painting using the information about colours and forms which he absorbed as he looked at the motif; the *sensations colorantes* perceived with his eyes, the prime outlet of his personality. He painted what he saw, and not what he knew. He saw nature in its raw, primaeval state, transmuting what he saw into a new reality borne of his own perceptions; he "realized" nature anew.

Cézanne once described his way of perceiving nature to the author Joachim Gasquet. He used the image of spread and closed fingers to explain his manner of reproducing a motif.

"This is what one must achieve. If I reach too high or too low, everything is a mess. There must not be a single loose strand, a single gap through which the tension, the light, the truth can escape. I have all the parts of my canvas under control simultaneously. If things are tending to diverge, I use my instincts and beliefs to bring them back together again… Everything that we

Paul Cézanne on the hill at Les Lauves in Aix, photographed in 1904 by Émile Bernard.

PAGE 66
Mont Sainte-Victoire, Seen from Les Lauves,
c. 1902–06
Watercolour and pencil, 47 x 30.7 cm
(18½ x 12 in.)
Philadelphia Museum of Art,
Gift of the families of Helen Tyson Madeira
and Charles R. Tyson

Lake Annecy, 1896
Oil on canvas, 64 x 79 cm (25¼ x 31 in.)
London, The Courtauld Institute of Art

Cézanne thought Lake Annecy, with its
dramatic mountain surroundings, was
almost too picturesque, suited "to drawing
exercises for young Englishwomen." In
his hands, the lake becomes an opaque area
of colour, and the sides of the mountains
are tectonic masses.

see disperses, fades away. Nature is always the same, even though its visible manifestations eventually cease to exist. Our art must shock nature into permanence, together with all the components and manifestations of change. Art must make nature eternal in our imagination. What lies behind the nature?

Nothing perhaps. Perhaps everything. Everything, you understand. So I close this errant hand. I take the tones of colour I see to my right and my left, here, there, everywhere, and I fix these gradations, I bring them together… They form lines, and become objects, rocks, trees, without my thinking about it. They acquire volume, they have an effect. When these masses and weights on my canvas correspond to the planes, and spots which I see in my mind and which we see with our eyes, then my canvas closes its fingers. It does not waver. It does not reach too high or too low. It is true, it is dense, it is full… But if I have the slightest distraction or feel the slightest weakness, particularly if I start reading too much into things, if I am swept along by a theory today which contradicts yesterday's, if I think when I am painting, if I interfere, then bang, everything slips away."

This newly created reality is centred on permanence and stability. It is very different from the temporal, unstable "Sunday celebration of the moment" which the Impressionists created in their paintings.

Cézanne's mother died in 1897. He had looked after her with great devotion during her final years, when she was frail and in need of care and attention. In order that her estate could be divided between the three children, the Jas de Bouffan, Cézanne's home for so many years, was sold. It is not known why Cézanne agreed to the sale; he could have afforded to buy out his sisters. The property may have been too large for him on his own, and his wife and son were living in Paris for most of the time. So Cézanne left the house, with its salon still containing the murals he had painted in his youth, with its grounds and magnificent avenue of chestnut trees, its old trees and its view of Mont Sainte-Victoire. He moved into an apartment in the centre of Aix, in the Rue Boulegon.

He took on a housekeeper, Madame Brémond. "I am under orders not to touch him," she told Cézanne's friend and biographer Émile Bernard, "not even with my dress when I go past him."

Mont Sainte-Victoire and Château Noir,
1904–06
Oil on canvas, 65.6 x 81 cm (26 x 32 in.)
Tokyo, Bridgestone Museum of Art,
Ishibashi Foundation

PAGE 70
In the Grounds of Château Noir, *c.* 1900–04
Oil on canvas, 90.7 x 71.4 cm (35¾ x 28 in.)
London, The National Gallery

The transformation and resolution of objects into areas of colour is a feature of Cézanne's later works. This view of painting no longer requires dramatic motifs: a randomly chosen detail of landscape containing tree trunks, foliage and block-shaped rocks suited Cézanne's distinctive ideas of pure painting just as well as the Château Noir or Mont Sainte-Victoire.

TOP
View of Château Noir, *c.* 1885
Oil on canvas, 73.5 x 92.5 cm (29 x 36½ in.)
Winterthur, Sammlung Oskar Reinhart
"Am Römerholz"

Cézanne depicts the "Black Castle," popularly believed to be a place where Satanic rituals were held, as a mysteriously glowing building hidden behind dense foliage.

Quarry at Bibémus, *c.* 1895
Oil on canvas, 65 x 81 cm (25½ x 32 in.)
Essen, Museum Folkwang

In the 1890s, Cézanne found new subjects east of Aix: the Château Noir and the quarry at Bibémus, whose reddish-ochre shell limestone had been used for building since Roman times. The strength of the painting comes from its chaotic jumble of rock faces drenched in sunlight. So powerful is their colour that it is even reflected by the sky.

Some years before, Cézanne had rented a small cottage near Bibémus quarry to the east of Aix to make it easier for him to paint in the open air, and he now began using this. He also rented a room in the Château Noir, an estate halfway to the village of Le Tholonet on the way to Mont Sainte-Victoire, where he could store his painting equipment.

The "black castle" was in fact a reddish roughcast neo-Gothic building belonging to a coal merchant who had come into some money. This was the place where Cézanne produced many of his late paintings; surrounded by pine forests, with the ochre-coloured stone of Bibémus quarry nearby and a view of the towering rockface of Mont Sainte-Victoire.

The mountain, a massive limestone ridge around a thousand metres high, fascinated Cézanne all his life and it provided an inexhaustible source of new compositions.

The early works containing mountain motifs include *The Great Pine* (*Mont Sainte-Victoire*, 1886/87, The Phillips Collection, Washington). Here, the mountain has not yet become the dominant motif in the painting but is an integral part of the landscape. The eye is led along the valley of the river Arc and its railway viaduct towards Mont Sainte-Victoire.

The landscape is framed by the trunks and branches of two stone pines serving as a foreground motif. Their flowing contours neatly follow those of the mountain itself, and the pale green of the valley floor, interspersed with patches of yellow ochre, is just as intense in the background as it is in the foreground.

The Great Pine has distance rather than any real depth; it is not three-dimensional in the traditional sense. Even the mountain, the most distant object in the picture, is darkly outlined, giving it a clear structure and spatial orientation. It is positioned above rather than behind the fields, between the valley floor and the stone pine branches.

As is so often the case with Cézanne's paintings, it is impossible to say what time of day, or what season, this picture depicts. The evergreen vegetation, the even, passionless light and the understated atmosphere make it impossible to ascribe it to a particular moment.

Mont Sainte-Victoire Seen from Bibémus,
c. 1897
Oil on canvas, 65 x 81 cm (25½ x 32 in.)
Baltimore Museum of Art,
The Cone Collection, formed by Dr. Claribel Cone and Miss Etta Cone of Baltimore

Mont Sainte-Victoire, Seen from Les Lauves,
1904–06
Oil on canvas, 73.8 x 81.5 cm (29 x 32 in.)
Kansas City, Missouri, The Nelson-Atkins
Museum of Art, Nelson Fund

It is as though Cézanne has removed any distractions which could make the subject of the painting unclear in any way, so that the reality of nature can speak for itself. This reality is not the reality of the moment, of a momentary "being thus," but rather one which embodies the experience of immutability and permanence, of simply "being there." This is what Cézanne meant when he said that he wanted to make Impressionism into something permanent, like art in museums.

Cézanne passionately directed all his efforts towards this end. He once said to Joachim Gasquet: "Impressionism, what does it mean? It is the optical mixing of colours, do you understand? The colours are broken down on the canvas and reassembled by the eye. We had to go through that. Monet's *Falaises* will always be a wonderful series of pictures, and so will a hundred other works by him… He has painted the gleaming iris of the earth. He has painted water… But now we need to give a firmness, a framework, to the evanescence of all things, and to these pictures by Monet."

Mont Sainte-Victoire, Seen from Les Lauves,
1904–06
Oil on canvas, 59.9 x 72.2 cm (23½ x 28½ in.)
Basle, Kunstmuseum Basel

Although spots of paint are still used to
represent areas of foliage or buildings, the
Sainte-Victoire paintings from the latter
part of Cézanne's life are increasingly
abstract. The sky seems to merge with the
foreground, particularly on the left-hand
side; the three-dimensionality of landscapes
before Cézanne seems to have disappeared.

Cézanne's concept of a fixed structure should not be understood as
depicting nature where time has stood still, frozen in a particular moment.
He is not trying to bring fixity to the paintings of the Impressionists.

His pictures aim instead at creating a permanence in the sense of
timelessness, but a timelessness that also embraces solidity and flux, order
and flexibility. As the art historian Gottfried Boehm put it in his monograph
on Cézanne's paintings of Mont Sainte-Victoire, the artist sought to achieve
a "synthesis of change and permanence, two identical sides of the same
visible manifestation."

So how did Cézanne achieve this? What method did he use to create a
visual representation of this ordered flexibility? We can begin to answer this
question by looking at his late paintings of Mont Sainte-Victoire (ill. pp. 66,
69, 73–79).

These show the mountain as the dominant motif of the landscape and
the painting, a grand, monumental geological formation. Like another

Mont Sainte-Victoire, Seen from Les Lauves,
c. 1904–06
Oil on canvas, 63.5 x 83 cm (25 x 32¾ in.)
Zurich, Kunsthaus Zürich

Cézanne has built up this composition using
individual spots of light and dark colour which
create the impression of landscape only when
they are juxtaposed. The sky contains the same
green as the ground, and the spots of white
unpainted canvas create an open feeling. These
white areas emphasize the two-dimensional
nature of the surface.

mountain in Provence, Mont Ventoux, Mont Sainte-Victoire has acquired
an almost mythical status in the Provençal mind.

When the Italian poet Petrarch climbed Mont Ventoux in the year 1335,
he experienced landscape in a completely new way. "At first I stood, moved
by an unfamiliar breath of wind and by a great panorama, like a man in
a daze. I looked back down; clouds lay at my feet, and I found it easier to believe what they say about Mount Athos and Mount Olympus, for I was
seeing on a lesser-known mountain what I had read and heard about them."

Cézanne showed the mountain from the Plateau d'Entremont, to the
west, from which the mountain resembles a cone falling off steeply to the
south. It stands before us, a powerful and immediate presence, with no
framing motif to divert the eye. Cézanne has built up the picture from small,
flat areas of paint. There is no feeling of movement or flow; the scene is one
of calm and tranquillity. The artist has treated the surface of the painting in
an exceptionally abstract way, placing dark areas of colour and man-made
structures apparently at random on the canvas.

Nothing in the individual areas of colour bears any specific relationship with the visible world of objects, and it is not possible to identify trees, fields or houses. Only the interaction between the different elements within the painting as a whole enables us to recognize an objective reality.

"Nature is not on the surface; it is in the depths. Colours are the surface expression of this depth. They grow up from the roots of the world. They are its life, the life of ideas."

To Cézanne, colours are the only constituent elements of an image. Its form is determined by the way they are applied; the boundaries between colours are also the boundaries between forms. The light in his paintings has no existence in its own right; it is created by the colour. "Light is not a thing that can be reproduced, but something that must be depicted using something else: colours."

This meant that Cézanne depicted the brightest and strongest light using the most intense colours rather than by using lighter ones. He used light and dark colours to create areas of light and shade, and he used contrasts of colour

Mont Sainte-Victoire, 1902–06
Oil on canvas, 64.8 x 81.3 cm (25½ x 32 in.)
Philadelphia Museum of Art,
Gift of Helen Tyson Madeira, 1977

to create the structure of his paintings. He spoke of the particular ability of blue to give breadth and height to a space or, as he put it, "to make the air tangible."

Anyone who has ever visited Provence will have experienced this phenomenon of light created by intense colours. The bright Provençal sun, deep blue sky and clear air are hazy only in the middle of the day. They bathe the landscape in saturated colour which has an almost unreal quality about it. The light brings out the maximum of colour from objects; things seem to have their own inner glow. Even an ordinary scree-covered hillside, a gravel path or a rock will absorb the colour of the surrounding vegetation and the sky, and glow with it.

In the Basle painting of *Mont Sainte-Victoire, Seen from Les Lauves* (1904–06, ill. p. 75), Cézanne uses an intense blue to depict light. It is a tran-scendently atmospheric colour, which also makes a brief appearance amid the shadows in the foreground, as though part of the light were breaking through the yellow ochre and green of the ground.

The shadow on either side of the brightly lit area is painted in dark violet tones mixed in with red and green. These are predominantly warm tones, creating a contrasting tension with the cool blue of the mountain. They also seem to be closer to the viewer, whereas the blues appear to be further away.

Cold and warm colours, closeness and distance are interwoven. But despite these inherent contrasts and tensions, the picture of Mont Sainte-Victoire is a balanced and self-contained framework of colours and forms. Change and permanence, order and flexibility are combined to create an extraordinary, virtuoso form of dynamic equilibrium.

In the Zurich version of *Mont Sainte-Victoire, Seen from Les Lauves* (1904–06, ill. p. 76), Cézanne has left areas of the composition unpainted and white. These may be areas which he has not sufficiently worked out in his mind; perhaps he has not yet managed to find the right colours for what were effectively areas of "no-man's land."

Although Cézanne's fellow artists – Monet, Pissarro, Sisley, Renoir – were showing an increasing appreciation of his work, his own emotions still fluc-tuated wildly between euphoria, depression and, in some cases, even despair.

In the spring of 1895 he asked the art critic Gustave Geffroy to sit for a portrait. After three months of daily sittings he gave up on the painting, say-ing apologetically to Geffroy that he had taken on too much, and returned despondently to Aix.

The same year, however, brought Paul Cézanne a personal triumph: the young art dealer Ambroise Vollard opened an exhibition of some fifty of his paintings in December 1895.

Vollard, who had his gallery in Rue Laffitte, had developed links with Cézanne through the artist's son Paul, now aged twenty-three. Paul was in-creasingly taking care of his father's business affairs and regularly sold paint-ings by Cézanne to Vollard, receiving an agency fee of ten per cent from both parties. "The boy is much smarter than I am," Cézanne said admiringly of his son, "I have no practical sense." Cézanne did not grow rich from the

Mont Sainte-Victoire, 1890–95
Oil on canvas, 55 x 65.4 cm (21¾ x 25¾ in.)
Edinburgh, National Galleries of Scotland

sale of the paintings, but Vollard did at least guarantee to take all of them, including those which were unfinished or damaged.

The art critic Gustave Geffroy wrote an article in praise of the exhibition at Vollard's gallery.

"Passers-by walking into the Galerie Vollard, in Rue Laffitte, will be faced with about fifty pictures: figures, landscapes, fruit, flowers, from which they can finally reach a verdict on one of the finest and greatest personalities of our time. Once that has happened, and it is high time that it did happen, all that is dark and legendary about Cézanne's life will disappear, and what remains will be a rigorous and yet attractive, masterly and yet naive life's work… He is a great fanatic for the truth, fiery and naive, austere and subtle. He will end up in the Louvre."

The Bathers – The Latter Years

After the Vollard exhibition, collectors became increasingly interested in Cézanne, and his paintings began to fetch significant prices at auction. Zola's collection was auctioned in September 1902 after his death from smoke poisoning, and one early picture, *The Abduction*, achieved a record price of 4,200 francs. A landscape by Monet, who was a much more respected artist, fetched only 2,805 francs.

But the majority of the press and public still had little sympathy for this new way of depicting nature. After the auction of Zola's paintings, a malicious article in *L'Intransigeant* strongly criticized both Cézanne and Zola as those "who propagated this madness with the brush." The article, by Henri Rochefort, a rival of Zola, provided further grist to the mill of public opinion in Aix; thousands of copies of *L'Intransigeant* were sent to Aix and distributed among conservative art lovers. Cézanne and his family received threatening letters, and the artist came more under fire than ever before from small-minded citizens who ideally would have liked to hound the eccentric banker's son out of town.

During the years that followed, Cézanne took part in an increasing number of exhibitions. He had three paintings on display at the Salon des Indépendants and the Paris World Exhibition in 1900, and his fame spread to neighbouring countries; the Berlin Nationalgalerie was the first gallery to acquire one of his paintings. He exhibited at the Vienna Secession and in Brussels and had a room to himself at the newly established Autumn Salon of 1904, containing thirty-three of his paintings.

Cézanne worked unstintingly. After the sale of the Jas de Bouffan, all that he had left was his small temporary studio in the Rue Boulegon and the rented rooms in the Château Noir. He tried to buy the château, but his offer was turned down by the owner. He therefore bought a plot of land on the Chemin des Lauves, on an otherwise undeveloped hillside to the north of Aix, and had a two-storey house built with a large studio, some five metres high, on the first floor. The outer wall of the studio had a long, narrow slit in it so that large canvases could be pushed through it (ill. p. 88 bottom).

Standing model, undated
New York, The Museum of Modern Art

PAGE 80
Man Standing, Hands on Hips, c. 1885
Oil on canvas, 127 x 96.8 cm (50 x 38 in.)
New York, The Museum of Modern Art,
Lillie P. Bliss Collection

Cézanne preferred using photographs or sketches rather than nude models because he felt uncomfortable in their presence. This painting, too, is based on a photograph. It is unusual for one of Cézanne's bathers to dominate the picture as much as this one does.

Cézanne moved into this house in 1902, but kept his apartment in the Rue Boulegon. He only ever went into his studio to paint, which he usually did early in the morning and then again in the late afternoon. When it became too hot, he would paint watercolours on the terrace, which was surrounded by bushes and small trees and had a magnificent view of the town of Aix. From time to time, local agricultural workers or his gardener Vallier would sit for him, for example for his painting *The Gardener* (*c.* 1906, ill. p. 65).

During the last years of his life, Cézanne set himself another objective. He decided to devote a number of large compositions to a motif he had painted at the beginning of his career as an artist: semi-abstract figures in a landscape.

Now, aged over sixty, Cézanne recalled the most carefree and happy time of his life when he would go out with his friends Zola and Baille, exploring the area around Aix and spending many hours on the banks of the river. He produced many drawings, watercolours and oil paintings of these bathing scenes, calling them *Idyll, Nudes on the Riverbank* or simply *Bathers*. In all, he produced some 140 drawings, sketches and paintings depicting this motif.

But it was not just the personal memories of his youthful friendship that spurred Cézanne to produce so many of these works. The reasons lay even

Bathers, 1892–94
Oil on canvas, 27 x 41 cm (10¾ x 16¼ in.)
Moscow, Pushkin Museum

deeper than that: Cézanne had a great respect for the Classical painters of Arcadian idylls who sought to unite man and nature in perfect harmony. "Imagine Poussin wholly reclaimed from nature," he said to Gasquet. "That is the Classicism which I am striving to achieve." However, Cézanne sought his harmonies not in the artificial forms of the ancients, as had the old masters whom he so much admired, but in nature itself, which reveals its richness of colour to the close, open-minded observer.

But the results on canvas still fell far short of Paul Cézanne's inner perceptions. He never really achieved his aim; he could only ever come close to it, and life was a constant process of struggling and searching. In 1906, five weeks before his death, he wrote to his son:

"Finally, I would like to say to you that as a painter I am becoming more clear-sighted in the face of nature, but it is always very hard for me to realize my perceptions. I cannot achieve the intensity which evolves before my eyes; I do not have that wonderful richness of colour which animates nature. Here, on the bank of the river, there are many different motifs; the same

Six Women, 1874/75
Oil on canvas, 38.1 x 46 cm (15 x 18 in.)
New York, The Metropolitan Museum of Art, Bequest of Joan Whitney Payson, 1975

Cézanne has avoided individualizing his figures: his interest lies in creating an artistic harmony between the figures and the landscape rather than in the figures themselves. The expressive distortions of forms influenced other painters of the time, and particularly the Fauvists.

Bathers, *c.* 1900
Watercolour and pencil, 13 x 21 cm (5 x 8¼ in.)
Tokyo, Bridgestone Museum of Art,
Ishibashi Foundation

The figures of the eight male bathers in this
scene have merged into one with the lively
background of vegetation.

subject, seen from a different angle, offers an extremely interesting subject
for a study, and one of such complexity that I believe I could work on it for
months without changing my position, simply by looking first to the right,
and then to the left."

When he painted his figures in landscapes, Cézanne used the many
studies he had made since the beginning of his career as an artist. Some of
these came from the École des Beaux-Arts in Aix, where life drawing was
obviously part of the course, or the Académie Suisse in Paris, where he regularly drew from the model. The most important sources of inspiration were
his repeated visits to the Louvre, where he made pencil studies of paintings
by Delacroix, Rubens, Raphael, Veronese, Michelangelo and Poussin, as well
as of Classical, Renaissance and Baroque sculptures.

Cézanne made frequent use of these sketches, along with illustrations
from his sisters' fashion magazines and, when he painted figures, reproduc-
tions from books. Francis Jourdain mentions an album entitled *Le Nu au
Musée du Louvre*, containing distinctly mediocre illustrations, which
Cézanne bought from a street kiosk in Paris. Obviously Cézanne could not
draw without a model, and he very often used sources such as these, despite
their poor quality. But drawing was never any more than a means to an end,
used to sketch out an idea or create the external form of a figure in motion.
The lines and forms of these pictures derived solely from colour.

He even regarded the Louvre purely as a source of information, "a good
reference work." Cézanne regarded nature as the true teacher, with all its

infinite variety of phenomena; it was nature that was mainly deserving
of study. But it was also possible to learn from the Classical artists, and
particularly the Venetians.

"It does not matter which of them you prefer," he told Joachim Gasquet,
"he should simply provide you with direction. Otherwise you are an imita-
tor. If you have a feel for nature, however it is acquired, and a few good
ideas, you are bound to achieve your own freedom; you must not let other
people's advice and methods change your own way of seeing things."

The theme of the bathers in Cézanne's work can be traced back to the
beginning of the 1870s. Male and female bathers rarely appear together in
the same painting, and these works are therefore very different from the
dramatic pictures of the 1860s and early 1870s, in which Cézanne used the
confrontation between the sexes in a provocative way. This is probably the
result of Cézanne's strong feeling of shame, his sexual inhibitions and fears,
and his shyness about showing naked men and women together in what he
regarded as trivial, sensual poses.

Cézanne's aim in strictly segregating the sexes in the *Bathers* series was
to exclude any connotations from the situation, any element of the transient,
sensual or erotic. This meant that his figures became internalized, spiritual
beings, and he could concentrate wholly on the purely formal, compositional
problems of his pictures because they had been freed of content.

Cézanne painted numerous watercolours on this theme. In the sheet
from a sketch album, *Bathers* (*c.* 1900, ill. p. 84), six of the men are clearly

Bathers, 1900–06
Watercolour and pencil, 13 x 21 cm (5 x 8¼ in.)
Private collection

Page from a sketchbook; the layout of the
landscape and the groups of figures bear simi-
larities to the version of *The Large Bathers* in
the Philadelphia Museum of Art.

visible, and two more, on the right of the picture, are suggested by a few curved outlines. These have melted into the background, which is full of movement, and are therefore at one with nature. It is a turbulent scene, and includes the motif of the figure folding its arms behind its head which appears in nearly all the pictures of bathers. It is a gesture of relaxation, of opening oneself up and offering oneself. In this particular case it is presenting an erection to the seated figure in the bottom left-hand corner.

The small page of *Bathers* (1900–06, ill. p. 85) also comes from one of Cézanne's sketchbooks. It is a watercolour version of an oil painting, with an arch-shaped background of vegetation. Alternatively, this may have been a study for what is probably Cézanne's best-known painting on this theme, *The Large Bathers* (1900–06, ill. p. 89), now in the Philadelphia Museum of Art. The conical outline in the background may represent Mont Sainte-Victoire, though this is not certain. Here again, the figures and vegetation are closely interwoven. The picture is a delicate, highly complex tissue of bold brushstrokes, spots of paint and transparent areas of colour. The forms are extremely lively and varied; light, open and insubstantial. The group of bathers and the vegetation have merged into a unity in which time no longer seems relevant. The picture seems to be expressing Cézanne's longing for an existence which is in harmony with nature, and in which humans bear strong affinities with the plant world that surrounds them.

There are few colours: a transcendent blue, bordering on violet, and a yellow which verges on yellow ochre and is mixed with the blue in the

The Large Bathers, 1895–1906
Oil on canvas, 132.4 x 219.1 cm (52¼ x 86¼ in.)
Philadelphia, The Barnes Foundation

The Large Bathers, *c.* 1894–1905
Oil on canvas, 127.2 x 196.1 cm (50 x 77¼ in.)
London, The National Gallery

areas of foliage to create a light green. But these combine with the pale background of the paper to create a very subtle and harmonious composition. The two groups of bathers on either side of the picture are not isolated from each other; they are enclosed by a natural stage, and linked together by spots of sunlight filtering through the leaves on the trees. The isolated figure in the bottom centre of the picture is reminiscent (but a mirror image) of the prostitute in Cézanne's painting *The Eternal Feminine* (*c.* 1877, ill. p. 36). Could this also be another memory of the confused sensuality of his early nudes?

The women in all the versions of the *Bathers* are anonymous creatures, with no personality or expression. They are archetypes; their form is more important to the artist than their individuality. Cézanne was primarily interested in the composition as a whole, the harmony between the figures and nature, and between form and colour.

Cézanne painted three large versions of the female bathers, all during the last seven years of his life. The version of *The Large Bathers* in the Philadelphia Museum of Art (1900–06, ill. p. 89) is the largest, at 210 x 250 cm. This was the first time that Cézanne had painted such a monumental canvas. It was for this painting, which of course was painted in the studio, that Cézanne had a slit built into the wall of his house so that he could also take

Cover page of the first monograph on Paul Cézanne, written in 1910 by Julius Meier-Graefe, with a drawing by Franz Marc.

A corner of Cézanne's studio on Chemin des Lauves. A partly completed painting stands on the easel, and behind it on the right is the slit in the wall that was constructed for *The Large Bathers*.

the painting outdoors and see it in natural daylight (ill. p. 88 bottom). The fact that the artist had himself photographed in front of another version of *The Large Bathers* (1895–1906, ill. p. 86), now owned by the Barnes Foundation in Philadelphia, when it was not yet complete shows how much importance he attached to this painting (ill. p. 95).

The figures in all three compositions are remarkably simply and coarsely painted. The female creatures frolicking on the riverbank are not graceful; rather they are sturdy, angular, oddly proportioned and plump, and have nothing erotic about them. Cézanne has avoided any suggestion of individuality or temporality and instead has generalized the figures in the same way as the landscapes, so that both have equal artistic weight.

In the Philadelphia version, the atmosphere is created by a light, transparent blue, whose effect is intensified by the complementary orange which is the other main colour. The two colours interact and intensify each other. The blue sky consists of glazing spots of paint which are mainly diagonal. It is made up of a number of layers, partly allowing the light-coloured ground of the painting to show through, and in some places is bound up with the green of the foliage. The blue covers most of the canvas, a turbulent and yet ordered lattice of colour. Superimposed on it is the powerful triangle created by the tree trunks, the figures, the riverbank and the river itself. The trees are bent together, forming a straight-sided arch or protecting roof over the heads of the bathing figures. The riverbank and the river are created using horizontal lines of colour, offsetting the dynamic network of colour and line created by the trees and the figures.

Unlike the watercolour of the female bathers, Cézanne has focused not on the shimmering leaves, but on the trunks which bear the weight of the trees. These create a framework which is both static and dynamic. The figures are also aligned in the same way as the trees; this is probably most apparent in the female figure on the far left, whose upper body and left leg are inclined at exactly the same angle as the tree trunk. However, the contours and arms of the other figures also echo the geometry of the framework.

The women are self-absorbed; they exist only for themselves. In the background, the eye is led to a line of trees and two brightly lit figures on the other side of the riverbank. Only the left-hand of the two figures at the centre of the composition is clearly apparent; it is a man standing with his arms folded looking across the river at the women.

Kurt Badt suggests that this faceless figure is the painter himself; that Cézanne, "beneath the strong, protecting church tower," is looking on at the scene of happiness and harmony from "a distance which can never be bridged." In the large paintings of bathers, Cézanne has expressed his concept of a new Arcadia, a harmonious unity between man and nature. The painter himself has no part in this harmony. By depicting the figures so crudely, and not making it clear what they are doing, he has stripped them of their individuality and rendered them timeless. They are not being placed on an idealistic pedestal; nor are they everyday, contemporary figures. Rather they are almost abstract beings, recreated for artistic ends, whose incompleteness and lack of clear purpose break with all the cherished myths of nineteenth-century art. They are paving the way for a new form of art in which composition, colour and form predominate, and which follows only its own inherent rules.

"I am working stubbornly; I see the Promised Land before me," wrote Cézanne to the art dealer Ambroise Vollard. "Will my fate be the same as that of the great leader of the Hebrews, or will I be able to enter that land?"

The Barnes Foundation version of *The Large Bathers* is said to have taken eleven years to paint. This is not the result of any uncertainty in its dating; Cézanne really did spend so long painting it. His extremely slow way of working and dissatisfaction with the results of his efforts led him to leave a number of paintings unfinished. He spent more than a year working on one still life with flowers for Vollard before giving up in discouragement.

Cézanne's health worsened as he grew older. Apart from his diabetes, he also suffered from depression, which was mainly manifested in a growing

The Large Bathers, 1900–06
Oil on canvas, 210.5 x 250.8 cm (83 x 98¾ in.)
Philadelphia Museum of Art,
Purchased with the W. P. Wilstach Fund, 1937

Cézanne spent more than six years working on this painting. The strict triangular composition makes it the most classical of this series. The standing figure on the left is placed at the same angle as the tree trunk. Matisse, who had learned from Cézanne that "a painting gains its power from the tones of colour," used a version of this figure as a model for his 1909 painting, *Bather*.

Bathers, 1900–06
Watercolour, 21 x 27 cm (8¼ x 10¾ in.)
Private collection

distrust of his fellow human beings and eventually in paranoia. His mood swayed between euphoria and despair, but he was delighted at the increasingly frequent visits from friends and admirers of his work. He felt that at last he was being taken seriously. In January 1905 he wrote to Roger Marx, the editor of the *Gazette des Beaux-Arts*:

"My age and my health will never allow me to realize the dream of art that I have been pursuing all my life. But I shall always be grateful to the intelligent amateurs who had – despite my own hesitations – the intuition of what I wanted to attempt for the renewal of my art. To my mind, one does not substitute oneself for the past; one merely adds a new link to its chain. With the temperament of a painter and an ideal of art – that is to say a conception of nature – sufficient means of expression would have been necessary to be intelligible to the general public and to occupy a decent place in the history of art."

The summer of 1906, Cézanne's last, was unusually hot. Aix was enveloped in a torrid, suffocating heatwave which drove Cézanne almost out of his mind. He had his palette taken to the banks of the river Arc, where it was slightly cooler, and on a small bridge there he painted a number of watercolours, including *The Bridge of Trois-Sautets* (*c.* 1906, ill. p. 91). The spots of colour representing the foliage are almost abstract. Only the tree trunk, which serves as a *repoussoir*, and the arch of the bridge suggest planes and depth. In some parts of this painting he did something which was rare in his watercolours: he added pencil lines over the spots of paint afterwards to give them a degree of structure. "The main thing is to create as rich a harmony as possible," he wrote to his son in Paris.

The autumn finally brought cooler weather and rain. On 15 October, Cézanne was painting outdoors when he was caught in a huge storm. He was left wet and cold for several hours until he was picked up by a vehicle and taken home, badly weakened. The next morning, he went out into his garden to work on his portrait of the gardener Vallier (1906), and also wrote an angry letter to his art materials supplier about a delivery of paint (ill. p. 94 top). But his condition worsened rapidly. His wife and son, who were notified of his illness by telegram, arrived too late. Cézanne died of pneumonia early in the morning of 22 October 1906.

The Bridge of Trois-Sautets, *c.* 1906
Pencil and watercolour, 21 x 27 cm
(8¼ x 10¾ in.)
Cincinnati, Art Museum, Gift of John J. Emery

In the hot summer of 1906, Cézanne frequently went to the banks of the river Arc. Here, in the shade of the trees, he painted colourful, semi-abstract watercolours, to which he later gave added structure using pencil lines.

Paul Cézanne 1839–1906
Life and Work

Paul Cézanne, *c.* 1861

Paul Cézanne, *c.* 1875

Cézanne (seated) with Camille Pissarro
in Pontoise, *c.* 1877

1839 Paul Cézanne is born on 19 January in Aix-en-Provence, the eldest of three children. His father, Louis-Auguste Cézanne, is a dealer and exporter of felt hats in Aix. His mother, Anne-Elisabeth Honorine Aubert, is the daughter of a wood-turner from Marseilles. Paul is baptized in the Sainte-Madeleine church; his parents do not marry until January 1844.

1852 Attends the Collège Bourbon (now Lycée Mignet). Here he befriends Émile Zola, whose father is managing a dam project in Aix, and Jean-Baptiste Baille. The three "Inseparables" make frequent trips into the countryside around Aix.

1859 In accordance with his father's wishes, Paul reluctantly begins a law course at Aix University. He is exempted from military service because his father pays for a substitute. Wins second prize for figure painting at the École spéciale de Dessin. Louis-Auguste Cézanne buys the Jas de Bouffan estate near Aix, the former summer residence of the Governor of Provence.

1861 Spends the period from April to the autumn in Paris and studies life drawing and painting at the Académie Suisse, where he also meets Camille Pissarro. Begins a portrait of Zola, which remains unfinished. In September, returns to Aix in a state of despondency and goes to work for his father's bank. He also attends the drawing school in Aix again.

1862 Sets up a studio at the Jas de Bouffan. Leaves the bank and his legal career and returns to Paris in November. His father pays him an allowance of 125 francs a month.

1863 Regularly works in the Académie Suisse during this and the following year. Here, in addition to Achille Empéraire and Pissarro, Cézanne meets Renoir, Monet and Sisley. His application to the École des Beaux-Arts is rejected on the grounds that, although he has the temperament of a colourist, his paintings are overdone.

1863 Cézanne's work appears along with that of Manet, Pissarro, Jongkind, Guillaumin, Whistler, Fantin-Latour and others in a "Salon

des Refusés." Paints wild, demonic, expressive pictures which are described as "flinging paint at the canvas." Regularly visits the Louvre and copies paintings by Delacroix.

1866 Rejected by the Salon, and writes a letter of protest to the Director of Fine Arts. Meets Manet, who praises his still lifes. First experiments with open-air painting. Goes to Aix from August onwards, where he paints a portrait of his father reading the newspaper.

1869 Rejected by the Salon again. Meets Hortense Fiquet, a 19-year-old bookbinder.

1870/71 Rejected by the Salon. Spends the period of the Franco-Prussian War with Hortense in L'Estaque. End of his dark, expressive, intuitive period. Returns to Paris after the Commune is declared.

PAGE 92
Cézanne at work, *c.* 1906

Cézanne's last letter, asking his paint dealer what has happened to the tubes of paint he ordered.
"Aix, 17 October 1906
Monsieur!
It is now eight days since I asked you to send me ten tubes of burnt lake 7, and I have had no reply. What is the matter?
A reply, and a quick one, I beg of you.
Yours faithfully,
Paul Cézanne"

1872 Cézanne's son Paul is born. The family moves to Auvers-sur-Oise, near Pontoise, where Cézanne works closely with his friend and mentor Pissarro.

1873 Befriends Dr Gachet, in whose house he paints. Meets the paint dealer Julien Tanguy and exchanges paint for pictures. Meets Van Gogh at Tanguy's house.

1874 At the studio of the photographer Nadar first group exhibition by the Impressionists Cézanne's paintings *(The House of the Hanged Man at Auvers, Landscape, Auvers, A Modern Olympia)* attract considerable attention. Spends the summer in Aix and returns to Paris in September.

1875 Rejected by the Salon. Through Renoir, meets the customs inspector and art-lover Victor Chocquet, who becomes one of the most enthusiastic collectors of his work. Auction of paintings in the Hôtel Drouot.

1877 Shows sixteen paintings at the third Impressionist exhibition and again provokes a hail of criticism.

1878 Spends the year in Aix and L'Estaque, while Hortense and their young son live in Marseilles. Cézanne's father learns of the family's existence and cuts Cézanne's monthly allowance. Zola helps him with his money problems. Rejected by the Salon.

1879 Rejected by the Salon. In August, visits Zola in Médan, but is alienated by his luxurious lifestyle.

1885 Rejected by the Salon again and decides not to enter any more pictures. Spends this and subsequent years mainly in Aix and the surrounding area.

1886 Breaks off friendship with Zola after publication of *L'Œuvre*, Zola's novel about a failed artist. Marries Hortense Fiquet. Cézanne's father dies in August, and he inherits a considerable fortune.

1887 Spent mainly in Aix. Paints with Renoir at the Jas de Bouffan.

1890 Shows three paintings at the "Les Vingt" exhibition in Brussels. In summer, spends five months with his family in Switzerland. Returns to Aix in autumn. Found to have diabetes.

1895 First one-man exhibition in December at the gallery of the Paris art dealer Ambroise Vollard.

1896 Paints in Bibémus quarry. Meets the writer Joachim Gasquet.

1897 Spends most of his time in Aix. His mother dies in October. The Nationalgalerie in Berlin is the first gallery to buy one of his paintings.

1898 Works in Aix, in the area and around the Château Noir. Later spends one last long period in Paris.

1899 Stays in Paris until the autumn, and then returns to Aix, where he remains almost continuously for five years. Jas de Bouffan sold.

Cézanne buys a small apartment in the town of Aix and takes on a housekeeper. His wife and son mainly live in Paris. Another one-man exhibition held at Vollard gallery; his paintings fetch significant prices.

1900 Three of his paintings shown at the "Century Exhibition" in Paris.
The art dealer Cassirer organizes a one-man exhibition in Berlin, but not one of his paintings is sold.

1901 Takes part in the "Salon des Indépendants" in Paris and also in exhibitions in Brussels and The Hague. Buys a plot of land on Chemin des Lauves, overlooking Aix.

1902 Moves into his studio house on Chemin des Lauves. Zola dies in September.

1903 When Zola's collection of paintings is auctioned, the works by Cézanne fetch an average of 1,500 francs. Takes part in the Vienna Secession exhibition. Pissarro dies.

1904 Émile Bernard visits Cézanne in Paris and watches him working. Travels to Paris for the Autumn Salon, where thirty of his paintings are on display. Second exhibition at Cassirer's in Berlin. Becomes increasingly reclusive and is weakened by his diabetes.

1905 Exhibits at the autumn Salon and the "Salon des Indépendants." The art dealer Durand-Ruel sends ten of his paintings to the Impressionists exhibition in London.

1906 Takes part in the autumn Salon. Also in the autumn, Cézanne is caught in a storm while painting and dies of pneumonia shortly afterwards, on 22 October. Buried at the St Pierre cemetery in Aix.

1907 Major retrospective of Cézanne's work at the Autumn Salon, featuring fifty-six of his paintings.

1954 Cézanne's studio house on Chemin des Lauves is opened to the public.

TOP
Cézanne in front of *The Large Bathers*, 1904

PAGE 94 BOTTOM LEFT AND RIGHT
Cézanne's studio in Aix-en-Provence,
c. 1900–02

Photo credits

The publishers are grateful to the galleries, archives and photographers involved for granting reproduction rights and for their help and support in producing this book. The following credits apply in addition to those already mentioned in the picture captions:

Archiv für Kunst und Geschichte, Berlin: 22, 51, 54, 58–59, 63, 69, 87

Artothek, Peissenberg: 21, 47 (Jochen Remmer), 49 (Josef S. Martin), 70 (Alexander Koch), 79 (Joachim Blauel)

Bildarchiv Preußischer Kulturbesitz, Berlin: 25, 65 (Lutz Braun), 72, 82 (Alexander Burkatovski)

Bridgeman Art Library, London: 12, 15, 17 (Lauros-Giraudon/Bridgeman Art Library), 57 (Giraudon/Bridgeman Art Library), 60, 61 (Lauros-Giraudon/Bridgeman Art Library), 62 (Giraudon/Bridgeman Art Library), 71

Bridgeman Images: 4, 29, 42, 94 bottom, 95

Martin Bühler, Basle: 75

Ute Edelmann, Hamburg: 23

Giraudon, Paris: 32

Luiz Hossaka, São Paulo: 44

The Museum of Modern Art, New York, Fotografie© 1995: 80, 81

Photo © Tallandies / Bridgeman Images: 2

Réunion des Musées Nationaux, Paris: 10, 11, 24, 37, 45.

Imprint

EACH AND EVERY TASCHEN BOOK PLANTS A SEED!

TASCHEN is a carbon neutral publisher. Each year, we offset our annual carbon emissions with carbon credits at the Instituto Terra, a reforestation program in Minas Gerais, Brazil, founded by Lélia and Sebastião Salgado. To find out more about this ecological partnership, please check: www.taschen.com/zerocarbon
Inspiration: unlimited. Carbon footprint: zero.

To stay informed about TASCHEN and our upcoming titles, please subscribe to our free magazine at www.taschen.com/magazine, follow us on Twitter, Instagram, and Facebook, or e-mail your questions to contact@taschen.com.

© 2016 TASCHEN GmbH
Hohenzollernring 53, D–50672 Köln
www.taschen.com

English translation: Phil Goddard in association with First Edition Translations Ltd., Cambridge, England
Design: Birgit Eichwede, Cologne
Production: Horst Neuzner, Cologne

Printed in Slovakia
ISBN 978-3-8365-3017-0

PAGE 2
Paul Cézanne on his way to paint near Auvers, c. 1874

PAGE 4
The Smoker, 1890–92
Oil on canvas, 92.5 x 73.5 cm (36½ x 29 in.)
St. Petersburg, Eremitage